# IOWA

## ART OF THE STATE

ART OF THE STATE

# IOWA

The Spirit of America

*Text by Diana Landau*

Harry N. Abrams, Inc., Publishers

NEW YORK

This book was prepared for publication at
Walking Stick Press, San Francisco

Project staff:
    Series Designer: Linda Herman
    Series Editor: Diana Landau

For Harry N. Abrams, Inc.:
    Series Editor: Ruth A. Peltason

Page 1: Iowa's 1996 sesquicentennial celebrated in a field of soybeans
    and oats on the Tom Schultz farm in Crescent, designed and
    photographed from the air by Michael Whye.
Page 2: Embroidered textile of a farm scene in Oskaloosa, by a Hmong
    needlework artist. These Laotian tribespeople are among Iowa's
    most recent immigrants. *Photo David Cavagnaro*

**Library of Congress Cataloging-in-Publication Data**

Landau, Diana, 1950–
    Iowa : the spirit of America state by state / by Diana Landau
        p.    cm. — (Art of the state)
      ISBN 0-8109-5550-4
      1. Iowa—Civilization—Pictorial works.    I. Title.    II. Series.
F622.I36    1998
977.7—dc21                       97–12018

Harry N. Abrams, Inc.
100 Fifth Avenue
New York, N.Y. 10011
www.abramsbooks.com

*In the Garden,* woodcut by Carl Homstad, 1993. *Courtesy of the artist*

# CONTENTS

*View of the Mississippi from Wyoming Hill,* by William E. L. Bunn, 1946. *Collection of the Muscatine Art Center*

*Is this heaven?*
*—No, it's Iowa.*

*Dialogue from* Field of Dreams

The movies are a good barometer of America's longings. To judge by the recent crop of films set in Iowa's fields and towns, we regard it as a place close to America's heart—if not a heaven on earth. The images we hold in mind are of gently rolling cornfields, baseball games at dusk, communal ceremonies like threshing dinners and quilting parties, band concerts in the town center, neighbors helping each other through tough times. Movies romanticize, yet in their portrayals of Iowa there's a large helping of truth.

Iowa embodies the agrarian traditions on which our nation was built, and which we still cherish. As one of its native writers notes, the values of "independence, integrity, hard work, thrift, and pride of ownership...form the ideological bedrock upon which Iowa's 150 years of statehood have accumulated, like a deposit of fertile prairie loam."

It all started with the land—"glorious, broad, free, soul-kindling country," as one settler described it. Here Iowa both fulfills and flouts its myth. Far from the flat, featureless expanse many imagine, the state rises from its eastern edge—the Mississippi—in lofty bluffs. Its eastern third was once part of the Northeast's primeval woodlands. Westward, the woods gave way to the state's defining landscape: the tallgrass prairie, whose fertile soil yielded riches beyond the pioneers' dreams. The word went out and farmers streamed in, setting a pattern of farms and small towns that firmly formed Iowa's character and culture.

Iowa's heritage of self-reliance and community spirit was forged early. Settlers began putting down roots soon after the United States acquired the land in 1803, but statehood didn't come until 1846. The first Free State formed out of the Louisiana Purchase, Iowa was strongly antislavery and pro-Union during the great mid-century conflict. The state grew by leaps and bounds in the last half of the nineteenth century; then its population leveled off and has stayed remarkably stable. Like other Midwestern states, it absorbed immigrants from many parts of Europe, and individual communities have retained their German, Dutch, or Bohemian roots.

Iowa's cultural life has always thrived on the same intimate scale as do its towns. Iowans eagerly welcome cultural events from the outside world, from the days of traveling Chautauquas to today's performing arts tours. Home-grown products include the renowned painter Grant Wood and an impressive crop of novelists, dramatists, and musicians. Literary readings, regional theater, band concerts, and folk-life festivals have long been part of the scene.

In the past, many Iowa artists have taken their talent out of state—sometimes for training, sometimes for good—a phenomenon blamed on the lack of a cultural metropolis like Chicago or New York. And until recently, Iowa has devoted scant attention to interpreting itself through the arts, at least in a self-celebratory way. Events, however, are conspiring to nudge Iowa closer to the cultural spotlight. Far from driving artists away, Iowa's pastoral landscapes and close-knit communities now lure many creative folk, who find it a refuge from urban stress. Hollywood, never slow to spot a trend, has discovered in Iowa a source of enduring American values, and Iowa's State Fair recently starred in a major Broadway revival of the musical so named. The 1996

*The Corn Parade,* mural by Orr C. Fisher for the Mount Ayr Post Office, 1941. *Photo Mike Jaeger*

observation of its sesquicentennial—150 years of statehood—gave Iowa a chance to swagger a bit, with art and music festivals springing up all over the horizon, and even a new symphony commissioned to the words of Iowa poets.

As Iowa grows into an ever more global culture, no doubt its arts, too, will expand in style and subject beyond the embrace of its river borders. But their strength, like that of Iowans themselves, will remain rooted in the land and in the state's pioneer heritage. The wail of Bix Beiderbecke's trumpet, echoing river traffic on the Mississippi; the rolling rhythms of Hamlin Garland's fiction; the ingenious forms of folk art crafted from farm tools; the simple, satisfying patterns of traditional needlework—these reveal the recurring themes of human life in this "heart" of the heartland. ✻

# IOWA

*"The Hawkeye State"*
29th State

*Date of Statehood*
DECEMBER 28, 1846

*Capital*
DES MOINES

*Bird*
EASTERN GOLDFINCH

*Flower*
WILD ROSE

*Tree*
OAK

*Stone*
GEODE

## "Our liberties we priz

Iowa's official emblems reflect the state's sturdy patriotism and enduring ties with the land. The oak, a staple of the state's eastern woodlands, has stood for steadfastness since time immemorial. The Eastern goldfinch is a cheerful, social seed-eater that thrives in Iowa's grain fields. Its flag, in all-American red, white, and blue, bears an eagle and the state's ringing motto, and its song, penned by a Civil War hero, celebrates the native land and waters. Agricultural symbols—a wheat field, sickle, and plow—take center stage on the state seal, surrounding a citizen soldier and his cabin, with the Mississippi flowing behind. ✱

**Wild rose and Eastern goldfinch**

Geode

# nd our rights we will maintain."

QUERCUS macrocarpa.

Iowa has never specified exactly what kind of oak is its official tree, or what species of wild rose. The state's most common oaks are the white oak and bur oak. *Above:* White oak, *Quercus macrocarpa*, engraving by Auguste Plée from the drawing by Pierre-Joseph Redouté. *New York Public Library*

### *"The Song of Iowa"*
*(sung to the tune of "Der Tannenbaum")*

You ask what land I love the best,
  Iowa, 'tis Iowa.
The fairest State of all the West,
  Iowa, O! Iowa.
From yonder Mississippi's stream
To where Missouri's waters gleam,
O! Fair it is as poet's dream,
  Iowa, in Iowa.

*Words by Adjutant S. H. M. Byers*

### *All-Iowa Chowder*

1 cup onion, diced
1 cup celery, diced
¼ cup butter or margarine
2 tablespoons flour
2 cups hot water
3 cups potatoes, diced
1 17-ounce can cream-style corn
2 bay leaves
⅛ teaspoon ginger
Salt and pepper
2 cups ham, diced
1½ cups evaporated milk
8 ounces cream cheese

1. Sauté onions and celery in butter.

2. Mix together flour and hot water; add to onion mixture. Stir until flour is even and liquid is thickened.

3. Add potatoes, corn, bay leaves, ginger, salt, pepper, and ham. Cook until potatoes are just soft.

4. Stir in evaporated milk and cream cheese. Heat until cream cheese is melted. Serve with corn bread.

*Kathi Pudzuvelis, Cedar Rapids*
Linn County Recorder

*Right:* Commemorative stamp honoring Iowa's centennial in 1946. *Stamp King Below:* Iowa's Capitol in Des Moines is an outstanding late-19th-century building. Its towering dome, leafed in 23-carat gold, can be seen for miles. *Photo Mike Whye*

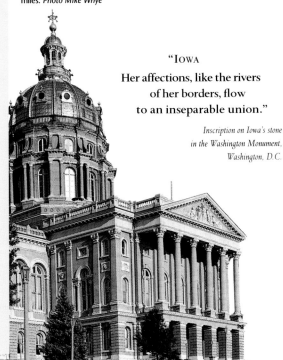

"IOWA
Her affections, like the rivers
of her borders, flow
to an inseparable union."

*Inscription on Iowa's stone
in the Washington Monument,
Washington, D.C.*

## "The Hawkeyes"

Theories abound about how Iowa was dubbed "The Hawkeye State" and Iowans "Hawkeyes," but the source is fairly well established. The pioneer lawyer David Rorer, wishing to avoid having an unflattering label attached to his fellow citizens, turned to the best-selling author of his day, James Fenimore Cooper, and his stalwart woodsman hero, Natty Bumppo, aka "Hawkeye." The name further resonates because it is shared by a truly heroic Iowan, the Sauk chief Black Hawk.

**"From all that is good, Iowa affords the best."**

*Early-20th-century slogan coined by
a Des Moines insurance company*

*Above:* Portrait of the
Sauk chief Black Hawk
by Charles Bird King,
c. 1837. *Hauberg Indian
Museum/Illinois Historic
Preservation Agency
Right:* License plate com-
memorating the 1996
sesquicentennial. *Iowa
Dept. of Transportation*

## Whence Came "Iowa"?

Both the state and the river got their name from a Native American tribe whom the Sioux called the Iowa. This name, filtered through the ears of early French explorers, has been variously translated as "dust-in-the-faces," "drowsy ones," "he who paints pictures," or more prosaically, "here is the place" and "beautiful land." It has been written in even more different ways:

*Ay-u-vois
Ayavois
Ay-u-ou-ez
Aiaoua
Ioway
Ayoüas
Ayoës
Ayoouois*

**c. 500 B.C.** Mound-building civilization thrives.

**1541** Hernando de Soto discovers Mississippi River.

**1673** Louis Jolliet and Father Jacques Marquette are first Europeans to set foot on Iowa soil.

**1682** Robert Cavalier, Sieur de la Salle, claims entire Mississippi Valley for France and names it Louisiana.

**1733** Sauk and Mesquakie Indians flee to Iowa after being forced out of Wisconsin by French.

**1762** France cedes Louisiana territory west of the Mississippi to Spain.

**1781** Lead is discovered in present-day Iowa.

**1788** Trader Julien Dubuque obtains permission from Mesquakie to work the lead mines.

**1801** Spain retrocedes western Louisiana territory to France.

**1803** United States purchases Louisiana, including Iowa country, from France.

**1804** Meriwether Lewis and William Clark traverse Iowa's western border on their ascent of the Missouri.

**1805** Territory of Louisiana, including Iowa country, established.

**1812** Congress makes Iowa region part of Missouri Territory.

**1820** Missouri Compromise makes Iowa region free territory.

**1821** Missouri's admission as a state leaves Iowa without civil government.

**1832** Black Hawk War ends with Indians ceding to the U.S. a strip of land west of the Mississippi known as the Black Hawk Purchase; permanent white settlement of Iowa begins.

**1834** Iowa made part of Territory of Michigan. Fort Des Moines established at confluence of Mississippi and Des Moines rivers.

**1836** Wisconsin Territory, including Iowa lands, established. Population of Iowa country: 10,564.

**1838** Territory of Iowa established; Robert Lucas appointed its first governor.

**1839** Iowa City becomes territorial capital; legislature sets up system of common schools.

**1840** Proposal for statehood defeated in referendum. Population 43,112.

**1846** Iowa enters the Union as the 29th state. Mormons migrate across southern Iowa.

**1847** University of Iowa, at Iowa City, is chartered.

**1850** Population 192,214.

**1855** Amana Colony founded in Iowa; university opens in Iowa City.

**1857** State capital moved from Iowa City to Des Moines; present state constitution adopted.

**1860** Population 674,913.

**1861** Civil War: Iowa sends 80,000 men to Union army during the war.

**1867** First railroad completed across the state, to Council Bluffs.

**1870** Population 1,194,020.

**1877** First telephone line built in Iowa.

**1887** First Corn Palace built at Sioux City. (One was built each year until 1891.)

**1890** Iowa becomes nation's leading producer of corn. Population 1,912,297.

**1891** Baseball World Series held in Sioux City.

**1898** Spanish-American War: Iowa infantrymen sent to Cuba and Philippines.

**1900** Population 2,231,853. "Good roads" movement begins.

**1911** Free high school education extended to all qualified pupils.

**1914** Iowa Art Guild organized.

**1917** World War I. Iowa national guard regiment goes to France.

**1919** WSUI in Iowa City, first radio station west of the Mississippi, begins broadcasting.

**1920** Population 2,404,021. Decline in farm prosperity begins.

**1928** Iowan Herbert Hoover elected president.

**1931** Susan Glaspell wins Pulitzer Prize in drama.

**1932** Art colony at Stone City founded.

**1940** Henry Wallace elected vice president under Roosevelt.

**1946** John Mott wins Nobel Peace Prize for his YMCA work.

**1956** Mackinlay Kantor wins Pulitzer Prize in fiction for *Andersonville*.

**1993** Massive flooding of the Mississippi, Missouri, and their tributaries causes many deaths and widespread loss of homes in Iowa.

**1996** Iowa celebrates its sesquicentennial (150th year as a state).

# "...that garden spot between the great rivers..."

Hugh Sidey, 1996

Iowa has been described as a Mesopotamia embraced by the continent's two chief rivers. Its eastern border is inscribed by the mighty Mississippi, while on the west, the Missouri divides Iowa from the true Plains states of Nebraska and South Dakota. All of Iowa's rivers are tributaries of one or the other, with most flowing east into the Father of Waters.

But before rivers could carve their way through the land, the land had to be created. Eons ago, shallow tropical seas occupied this part of North America, advancing and receding in stages, leaving behind layer upon layer of rock-forming sediments. Later, glaciers descended from the subarctic realm, scraping the land flat in places, gathering rocks into mounds and ridges in others. Frigid, ice-born winds lifted fine silt from valleys and scattered it far and wide, most notably in the northwestern region called the Loess Hills.

Iowa's subtly varied topography is the legacy of these forces. The nearly level western third is the state's most productive farmland, where fields and roads follow the old grid pattern laid out for homesteading. But southern Iowa

*Opposite:* Detail of a hydrographic map of the upper Mississippi basin from the surveys of Joseph Nicollet, engraved by William J. Stone, 1843. The earliest accurate map of the region, it shows the Iowa Territory occupying the upper two-thirds of the area between the two rivers. At the bottom, the Mississippi and the Missouri join—just north of St. Louis. *National Archives. Left:* Sugar maples in Pikes Peak State Park, Clayton County, overlooking the Mississippi River in northeastern Iowa. *Photo Carl Kurtz*

is rolling, rockier, and drier; agriculture is more challenging here. The state's northeastern corner—known as "Little Switzerland" for its steep hills and cliffs—is the only part untouched by the Ice Age. ✳

*View on the Missouri,* watercolor by Karl Bodmer, 1833. Although the exact location is not specified, this scene may well be set in Iowa. Bodmer accompanied Prince Maximilian of Wied on a historic expedition up the Missouri in 1832–33. *Joslyn Art Museum*

"[I REMEMBER IOWA AT MUSCATINE] for its summer sunsets. I have never seen any, on either side of the ocean, that equaled them. They used the broad, smooth river as a canvas, and painted on it every imaginable dream of color."

*Mark Twain,* Life on the Mississippi, *1883*

"THE FLAT VALLEY OF THE RIVER, about six or seven miles in breadth, is partly prairie, but interspersed with clumps of the finest trees, through the intervals of which could be seen the majestic but muddy Missouri."

*English naturalist John Bradbury, who explored the Missouri with the Astor expedition in 1811*

# WOODLAND AND PRAIRIE

Most of Iowa's early settlers got themselves, their families, farm equipment, and animals to the fertile prairie in Conestoga wagons. Rugged, versatile, and easily repaired, the Conestoga was the ubiquitous working vehicle of the frontier. *Opposite:* From a Currier & Ives print *Prairie Fires of the Great West,* this scene shows the Union Pacific Railroad in 1871, steaming through the prairie just ahead of the blaze.

**I**n primeval Iowa, the easterly lands were wooded, part of the great canopy of mixed hardwood forest that stretched from the Atlantic Ocean to the plains. Fringing the deep woods were flower-strewn meadows overspread with great oaks; these woodlands were rich in game.

Where the groves ended, the tallgrass prairie began—a unique ecosystem distinct from the shortgrass plains farther west. Early settlers marveled at this "sea" of grasses waving in the wind, high enough in places to hide a mounted rider, green in summer and decorated with a gorgeous array of wildflowers, golden in fall. Buffalo still ranged here into the 19th century, along with pronghorn, wolves, and countless small mammals and birds. The forests were cut for building timbers and shipped down the rivers; the prairie—30 million acres of it—was broken by the plow and transformed into an agricultural promised land. Only remnants of primeval Iowa linger today, in woodland and prairie preserves, or as isolated

clumps of grass and wildflowers along farm lanes. But Iowans are holding on to what's left of their natural heritage as stubbornly as they once strove to tame nature, treasuring these reminders of the earth they have always depended on. ✻

### The Pioneers

In bounds and darts the lighted grasses go;
  Leaps to its start the dreaded *prairie fire*,
In long, long lines the burning billows glow,
  Roars the night wind, the flames are leaping....

*Samuel Byers,* The Pioneers, *1896*

# *"The land is one of great beauty....*

It may be represented as one grand rolling prairie, along one side of which flows the mightiest river in the world, and through which numerous navigable streams pursue their devious way toward the ocean...."

*Albert M. Lea, c. 1840*

"OUR IMMEDIATE ANCESTORS CAME FROM LANDS COVERED WITH wood, and in their minds the idea of a wilderness was indissolubly connected with that of a forest....As they proceeded to the west, they found the shadows of the heavy foliage deepening their path, and the luxuriant forest becoming at every step more stately and intense...until suddenly the glories of the prairie burst upon their enraptured gaze, with its widely extended landscape, its verdure, its flowers, its picturesque groves, and all its exquisite variety of mellow shade and sunny light."

*Judge Hall, a mid-19th-century traveler, in*
Sketches of Iowa and Wisconsin,
*by John H. Plumbe (c. 1838),*
*an ardent booster of Iowa settlement*

**The low, or pasture, rose (***Rosa virginiana***) is an Iowa native.** *New York State Museum. Opposite:* **Big-tooth sunflowers, Indian grass, and trees at Prairie Creek Wildlife Refuge in central Iowa, a remnant of the primeval tallgrass prairie.** *Photo Carl Kurtz*

"AT FIRST WHEN WE WERE TOLD OF THESE TREELESS LANDS, I IMAGINED THAT IT WAS a country ravaged by fire, where the soil was so poor that it could produce nothing. But we have certainly observed the contrary: and no better soil can be found either for corn, or for vines, or for any other fruit whatever."

*Father Marquette, c. 1675*

*Spring on the Missouri* by Thomas Hart Benton, 1945. *North Carolina Museum of Art © Benton Trusts/VAGA, NY. Opposite above:* Sunset light on thunderheads. *Photo Carl Kurtz. Opposite below:* Whirlywheel by Milo Benda, c. 1980.

Though Iowa occupies latitudes where the climate is technically "temperate," anyone who lives there knows that the state's character owes much to its dramatic weather. Continental geography is the main reason: the Rockies and the Appalachians between them channel air masses from the north and the south, which tend to collide violently in the Midwest. Central North America, of which Iowa is the heart, endures more tornadoes than any other place in the world. And the word "blizzard," though not invented in Iowa, was used there for the first time in 1870 to describe a wind-driven snowstorm. On summer days, fields and farmers alike may wilt under fierce heat, and in springtime the Mississippi and its tributary rivers often rise and spill over in devastating floods. ✳

"THE WEATHER ISN'T ALWAYS EXTREME here; it just seems like it…"

*Anonymous*

"HOUSE ALL BROKE; toys all broke; but birds all working."

*Child's remark after a devastating tornado*

## How's the Weather?

Iowa has long, hot, moist summers and harsh, cold winters. Temperatures average 75°F in July and 19°F in January. Unpredictable winds can change local temperatures 50°F in a 24-hour period. Iowa's hottest day was in Keokuk in 1934, when the temperature reached 118°F; the record cold mark of -47°F was set in Washta in 1912. The heaviest recorded rainfall was in 1851: 74.5 inches in Muscatine.

**H**umans came to the land now called Iowa around 12,000 years ago, in the wake of the last glaciers. These Paleo-Indian people hunted mammoths and bison, along with smaller game; the only remaining trace of them is a few sharp-edged spear points. Later, some 8,500 years ago, came nomadic hunters of the Archaic period, and then the Woodland Indians, who occupied the upper Mississippi valley starting perhaps 4,000 years ago. The last group left traces of their culture along the river's west bank in Iowa's famed Effigy Mounds, where the dead were interred with their possessions in rock-and-earth berms often shaped

Rock art from the prehistoric Woodland culture of a human in a thunderbird costume, Allamakee County, Iowa.

like animals or people. These ancient peoples may or may not be ancestors of the six major tribes living on the land when Europeans arrived. They include the Sac (Sauk) and Fox (or Mesquakie, "people of the red earth") in the eastern region; the Iowa(y) (a Siouan tribe), the Potawatomie, and the Winnebago. Dakota Sioux also ranged into the northwestern Iowa territory. Like Native Americans everywhere, the Iowa tribes were pushed aside, dispossessed, and depopulated by the white invasion. In that story of conquest, major roles were played by the Sauk leaders Black Hawk and Keokuk, who lent his name to a city on the Mississippi. ✱

*Above:* Aerial view of the Great Bear Mound Group, Effigy Mounds National Monument, near Marquette. Effigy mounds, the work of the late Woodland culture, took the forms of humans, or animals, apparently chosen by ritual. The builders drew an outline with clamshells, then filled in the mounds with earth. *Photo National Park Service. Right:* Bear claw necklace, possibly from a Jones County, Iowa, site called Horsethief Cave, excavated in 1922. *University of Iowa, State Archeologist*

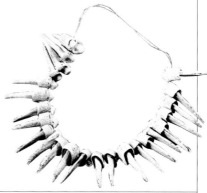

*Little Wolf, a famous warrior* by George Catlin, 1844. One of Catlin's most acclaimed Indian portraits, this was painted in a London studio. Catlin had recruited a troupe of fourteen Iowa and brought them to Europe, where they danced and performed *tableaux vivants* to promote his Indian Gallery. Notables from Benjamin Disraeli to George Sand flocked to meet the Iowa, but the venture abroad ended unhappily for Little Wolf with the death of his wife and child. *National Museum of American Art/Art Resource*

"MY REASON TEACHES ME THAT LAND CANNOT BE SOLD. THE GREAT SPIRIT GIVES IT to his children to live upon, and cultivate, as far as it is necessary for their subsistence; and so long as they occupy and cultivate it, they have the right to the soil.... Nothing can be sold but such things as can be carried away."

*From* The Autobiography of Black Hawk, *1834*

## Black Hawk's War

The powerful Sauk tribe was based in western Illinois, ranging into eastern Iowa to hunt and gather supplies. Told by the federal government in 1829 that they must move west of the Mississippi for good, most went without violence, but the respected chief Black Hawk objected, and in 1832 tried to reclaim his Illinois village. The army pursued him and his band for several months, finally forcing his surrender in Wisconsin. Thus ended the Black Hawk War; to punish the Sauk, the United States demanded they cede a 50-mile-wide swath of eastern Iowa, since known as the Black Hawk Purchase and quickly occupied by settlers.

*Above:* Mesquakie miniature cradle with human effigy, c. 1900, made of wood, bone, German silver brooches, leather, paint, glass beads, wool, and printed cotton cloth. The Mesquakie crafted beautiful objects from trade goods. *University of Iowa Museum of Art.* Left: Keokuk on Horseback by George Catlin, 1834. *National Museum of American Art/Art Resource*

*Right:* Mesquakie decorated cuffs owned by Gerald "Tuffy" Svacina, c. 1925, made of glass beads, cotton, and leather. *University of Iowa Museum of Art. Below:* Detail of silk appliqué sash, made by Mesquakie women for ceremonial occasions. *Iowa State Historical Society*

LONG AGO A CHILD, WHEN VERY YOUNG, OBSERVED A CERTAIN star in the heavens, which he regarded more than all the others. As he grew up, his attachment for the star increased, and his mind became more and more set upon it. When able, he went out to hunt, and while traveling, weary and alone, not having very good success, this favorite star came down to him and conversed with him, and conducted him to a place where he found bear and plenty of game. After this he was always a great hunter.

*Ioway Indian story*

"'YOU MAY NOW TRY TO SEW BEAD AND APPLIQUÉ RIBBON WORK. If you know how to sew you are to make things to wear when you dance. If it is known that you can already sew, [people] will hire you. Not merely that. You will be paid. You will be benefited by knowing how to sew,' my mother told me. Then indeed I began to practice sewing. It took me a long time to sew well. From then I was always making something."

Autobiography of a Fox Indian Woman, *translated by Truman Michelson, 1918*

somewhere inside me
there is a memory
of my grandfathers stalking
and catching robins
in the night of early
spring for food.
the snow continues
to gather children
outside, and i think,
as long as they are moving.
the frost sets itself
on the window before
the old man's eye.
we sit together
and imagine designs
which will eventually
vanish when the room
and talk become warm.
he goes over the people.
one by one…

*Ray Young Bear (Mesquakie)*
*from "Coming Back Home,"* 1980

*John Painter, Wife and Child, Mesquakie,* c. 1890, photographer
unknown, collected by Duren Ward. *Iowa State Historical Society*
Of all Iowa's tribes, only the Mesquakie still live in their native land.
A band of 80 Mesquakie refused to move to Kansas with the rest of
the tribe in the 1830s, instead purchasing a plot of land along the
Iowa River in Tama County, where many still live.

DISCOVERY OF THE MISSISSIPPI BY MARQUETTE, A·D·1673.

Marquette and Jolliet, exploring the Mississippi in 1673, met a party of Illini who had crossed the river to hunt on its western shores—that is, Iowa. Illustration by J. N. Marchand, 1903. *National Archives of Canada*

The French explorers Marquette and Jolliet in 1673 became the first Europeans to set foot on Iowa soil. As they entered the Mississippi from the Wisconsin River, near Iowa's present northern border, they admired the high bluffs on the western shore, then landed and trekked inland for a brief meeting with local Indians. Another French friar, Father Hennepin, pushed farther north on the Mississippi a few years later. Over the next century French traders entered the land between the rivers to trade with the Indians, but never attempted to farm or fortify it. Things changed dramatically after 1803, when the young United States acquired a vast expanse of new territory in the Louisiana Purchase. Lieutenant Zebulon Pike was dispatched in 1805 to trace the western tributaries of the Mississippi; he went up the Des Moines River as far as the camp of the Sauk chief Black Hawk (near present-day Burlington). Before long a trickle and then a flood of farmers and settlers poured through the Appalachians and across the Father of Waters, pushing the frontier—and the Indians—before them. ✱

Engraving of American explorer Zebulon Pike (1779–1813). *Corbis-Bettmann. Below: Various Points* by Genie Hudson Patrick, 1995. *Courtesy of the artist*

"THE SITUATION OF OUR LAST camp *councile bluff* or Handsom Prarie, (25 days from this to Santafee) appears to be a verry proper place for a Tradeing establishment & fortification. The Soil of the Bluff well adapted for Brick, Great deel of timber above in the two Points. . . . The air is pure and helthy so far as we can judge."

*Journal of Meriwether Lewis,*
*on the Lewis & Clark Expedition's*
*visit to Council Bluffs*

*River otter* by John James Audubon, c. 1839–48. The artist visited the Iowa country when the prairie was still intact, staying at a Potawatomie reservation in what is now southwest Iowa. *Opposite: Engineer Cantonment with Deer*, watercolor by Titian Ramsay Peale, 1822. *Iowa State Historical Society. Opposite below: Stephen Harriman Long* by Charles Willson Peale, 1819. Major Long led the first official expedition to the Iowa territory. *Independence National Historical Park*

That possession perhaps would come later, but in the meantime there were crops to plant, towns to plat, births, weddings and funerals to attend to. New graves to join those ancient mounds, shaped like the bear, the bird, and the lizard. The grasslands had become Iowa, the terra incognita had moved out of legend into the white man's geography and history books."

*Joseph Frazier Wall*, Iowa: A Bicentennial History, *1978*

## Limning the Territory

Among the notables who crossed the Iowa country early in the 19th century were several of America's leading artists of the period. George Catlin, the great painter of American Indians, spent some months in the 1830s living with the Sauk and the Mesquakie, and produced lively portraits of chiefs, warriors, and women in their distinctive dress. Journeys of exploration brought two other painters of note: Karl Bodmer, who accompanied Prince Maximilian of Wied on his voyage up the Missouri, and Titian Ramsay Peale, the Maryland-born artist who documented the Stephen Long expedition of the 1820s. And the indefatigable John James

Audubon visited and sketched at a Potawatomie Indian reservation in southwestern Iowa, recording bird and animal life, including the otters that still inhabit some of Iowa's rivers.

"ON THE UPPER MISSISSIPPI AND MISSOURI FOR THE distance of eight hundred miles above St. Louis is one of the most beautiful champaign countries in the world, continually alternating into timber and fields of the softest green....This is certainly the richest section of country on the continent."

*George Catlin, c. 1834*

In 1832, not more than 50 white people lived within the Iowa country, but during the next eight years the number of settlers swelled to 43,000. In 1838 the Territory of Iowa was officially established, with the territorial capital at Iowa City. Over the next decade, Iowans voted down statehood several times, but by 1846 they were ready to join the Union.

Iowa became a state at a time of social and political ferment. Reformers and religious crusaders of many stripes were active in eastern cities and on the frontier. The year 1846 also saw the Mormons blaze a trail across Iowa during their great migration westward; many stayed for years and left their mark on the state. And the searing political issue of the day—slavery—shadowed all affairs of state in the decades leading up to the nation's watershed conflict, the Civil War. ✳

*Flatboat on the Mississippi at Warsaw, Iowa,* litho-graph by Henry Lewis, c. 1846–47. From Lewis's *Mississippi Views.* Before the advent of steam, settlers relied on these human-powered craft to transport goods up and down the Midwest's waterways. *Iowa State Historical Society*

## "Wanted—thirty-seven thousand five hundred farmers!...

Let the news be scattered. Let the home-hunting immigrant be informed that a free home awaits him in Iowa."

*Headline in the* Waterloo Courier, *1868*

*American Progress* by John Gast, c. 1850. Throughout the 1830s and '40s, the wagons of westward-bound settlers wended their way in droves across the Iowa prairie. *Autry Museum of Western Heritage*

## Freedom and Union

In the mid-19th century, Iowa was growing fast and asserting itself on the national scene. The Mexican War began in the same year as statehood, and many Iowa place names refer to that war and its leaders. Some of the state's important schools were founded in the 1840s, inaugurating a strong tradition of higher education. The 1850s saw the first waves of European immigrants: Czechs, Dutch, Danes, French, and Germans.

Iowa played a major role in the antislavery crusade, partly because many Quakers lived there. Iowans operated outposts on the Underground Railroad, and John Brown maintained headquarters in the state for his followers. In the Civil War, Iowa supplied the Union with 80,000 troops, who fought with distinction at Shiloh, Vicksburg, and other battles. Though it boasts no famous commanders, two Iowans left lasting legacies: Mrs. Annie Wittenmyer, who put kitchens in military hospitals, and Adjutant S. H. M. Byers, the composer of "Sherman Marched Down to the Sea" as well as the official "Song of Iowa." On the facing page, he tells how the latter came about.

John Brown (1800–1859), in a painting by Balling, c. 1850. *The Bettmann Archive. Below:* The Eleventh Iowa Infantry Band, 1863. *Iowa State Historical Society*

The Todd House in Tabor, Iowa, home of Rev. John Todd, served as a station on the Underground Railroad. It was built in 1853 of native oak, cottonwood, and black walnut. Sketch by William Wagner. *Tabor Historical Society*

"WITH A SLAVE STATE ON OUR WESTERN BORDER, I SEE NOTHING but trouble and darkness in the future....With the blessing of God, I will war and war continually against the abandonment to slavery of a single foot of soil now consecrated to freedom."

*James Grimes, Whig candidate for governor of Iowa in 1854*

"AT THE GREAT BATTLE OF LOOKOUT MOUNTAIN, I was captured in a charge, and taken to Libby Prison, Richmond, Va. I was there seven months in one room....The rebel bands often passed the prison, and for our dis- comfiture, sometimes played the tune 'My Maryland' set to southern and bitter words. Hearing it once through our barred windows, I said to myself, 'I would like some day to put that tune to loyal words.'"

*Adjutant S. H. M. Byers*

### RUN AWAY ON SUNDAY

the thirty first of May 1846 from the subscriber, living in Waterloo Clark Co., Mo., a negro woman named Lucy about 36 years old, very stout and heavy made, very black, very large feet and hands, had on when she left a blue calico dress and a sunbonnet, no other clothing. It is believed that she will be conducted to the territory of Iowa...to a settle- ment of free negroes...

*Advertisement placed by a Missouri slaveowner*

*"It looks good enough to eat without putting it through vegetables."*

Robert Frost, on the soil of Iowa

Scenic view southward along the Loess Hills from the top of Murray Hill, Monona County, western Iowa. Loess, a fine glacial silt scattered during the Ice Age, augments the soil's fertility in this part of the state. *Photo Carl Kurtz*

**E**uropeans were not the first to farm Iowa—Native Americans of various tribes grew corn and beans, as well as hunting the woods and fishing the rivers—but the settlers raised agriculture to an art. At first the newcomers clung to the forests and river valleys, wary of the wide-open prairie with its fierce winds and fires. But when they discovered what riches lay beneath its cloak of head-high grasses and wildflowers—soils undisturbed for millennia, fed by the buffalo and deeply laced with roots—the prairie was quickly occupied and Iowa's history as a republic of farmers began to unfold.

Through the decades, Iowa farmers persisted in the face of storm, drought, flood, and insect plagues to make this prime land yield record crops. While farming no longer dominates every corner of the Iowa's economy, agrarian lifeways still set the tone for the state. ✳

"PRIOR TO THIS TIME I HAD BEEN COURTING THE COUNTRY; now I was to be united with it in that holy wedlock which binds the farmer to the soil he tills. Out of this black loam was to come my own flesh and blood, and the bodies, and I believe, in some measure, the souls of my children. Some dim conception of this made me draw in a deep, deep breath of the fresh prairie air."

*Herbert Quick,* Vandemark's Folly, *1922*

*Corn Country* by Lee Allen, 1937. Born in Muscatine in 1910, Allen was among the painters who carried out Grant Wood's designs for the library mural at Iowa State University. *University of Iowa Museum of Art*

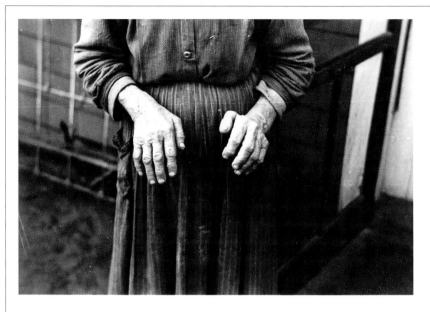

## Agrarian Attractions

Learn about farms in Iowa history, buy seeds, and taste old-time varieties, on visits to:

**Living History Farms**
Historical re-creations of Iowa farming from Indian times; in Urbandale. 515-278-5286

**Seed Savers Exchange and Heritage Farm**
2,000 heirloom vegetables and over 800 old-time apple trees; in Decorah. 319-382-5990

## The Farm in Art

Not surprisingly, Iowa's cultural creations often center on farm life and landscapes. Long before Iowa rural life was celebrated on film, it was immortalized on the canvases of its all-American painter, Grant Wood, and on the lively murals created for public buildings around the state by artists of the WPA. Novelists like Hamlin Garland, Herbert Quick, and Ruth Suckow made careers of hymning or exorcising their farm backgrounds. And contemporary Iowa poets, including James Hearst and Mary Swander, weave into their work the themes of families and communities close to the land.

"'I HATE FARM LIFE,' SHE WENT ON WITH A BITTER INFLECTION. 'It's nothing but fret, fret, and work the whole time, never going any place, never seeing anybody but a lot of neighbors, just as big fools as you are. I spend my time fighting flies and washing dishes and churning. I'm sick of it all.'"

*Hamlin Garland, "Lucretia Burns," 1891*

### Landscape—Iowa

No one who lives here
knows how to tell the stranger
what it's like, the land I mean,
farms all gently rolling,
squared off by roads and fences,
creased by streams, stubbled with groves,
a land not known by mountain's height
or tides of either ocean.
a land in its working clothes,
sweaty with dew, thick-skinned loam,
a match for the men who work it,
breathes dust and pollen, wears furrows
and meadows, endures drought and flood.
Muscles swell and bulge in horizons
of corn, lakes of purple alfalfa,
a land drunk on spring promises,
half-crazed with growth—I can no more
tell the secrets of its dark depths
than I can count the banners in a
farmer's eye at spring planting.

*James Hearst, 1979*

*Opposite: Hands of Mrs. Andrew Ostermeyer,* photograph by Russell Lee, 1936. *Library of Congress.* Top: Hand-carved wooden spoons by Erik Tiegen. *Vesterheim Norwegian-American Museum* Below: Halloween hay-bale sculpture in northwestern Iowa. *Photo David Thoreson*

## Beautiful Barns

Farm folk in Iowa frequently express their artistic impulses and love of place by creatively embellishing their environments. Barns, fences, and corncribs are painted with images ranging from American flags to the Mona Lisa to Miss Piggy, as well as trompe-l'oeil landscapes and farm animals. One young artist re-created Grant Wood's

*American Gothic* on his parents' corncrib.

Mailboxes, despite restrictions by the Postal Service, are favored canvases as well. And the farmers' ingenuity is often expressed in weathervanes, whirligigs, and gates made from old tools or parts.

The Duane Haley family of rural Sac City raises Simmental cows, one of which was rendered on a fence by their artistic daughter. *Photo Le Spearman*

## Landmarks in Cultivation

Iowa has pioneered agricultural innovations that changed food-growing around the world. Hybrid corn, which increases yields per acre manyfold, was developed here in the 1920s by Henry A. Wallace, whose father and grandfather were the editors of *Wallaces' Farmer,* and who later became U.S. Secretary of Agriculture. Another Iowan, John Froelich, built the world's first working tractor in 1892. The Delicious apple, now associated with the Northwest, was actually propagated in 1872 by Madison County orchardist Jesse Hiatt, who called it the "Hawkeye." Iowa continues to lead the way in food production, ranking first in the nation in corn, beef, pork, soybeans, and grain.

*Opposite:* This barn in Fort Dodge, now owned by Steve Friesth, was painted with the stars and stripes during the 1976 Bicentennial celebration; it was once used as a theater. *Photo Le* Spearman. *Above:* Stark-crimson Delicious apple, color illustration by Marilena Pistoia. *Arnoldo Mondadori Publisher. Right: Some Pig,* photo by David Cavagnaro

# "Corn, the most American

The state of Iowa was represented at the Sesquicentennial of 1926 in Philadelphia by a group of "Iowa corn folk" designed by Bertha M. H. Shambaugh and made from real corn.

**I**owa's coat of arms, suggests one writer, "should be a well-filled ear of corn." The ancient grain was cultivated and celebrated here long before European farmers arrived, and to this day sustains the state's agricultural prestige. The Corn Belt's wealth starts with its incredibly fertile soil, a gift of the Ice Age glaciers. Iowa, with just 1.6 percent of the U.S. land area, boasts 25 percent of its Grade A topsoil and leads the states in annual corn production with 900 million bushels. All kinds of corn are grown: tender sweet corn, corn for milling into meal, but mostly corn to feed through livestock, the other mainstay of Iowa's economy. In 1959, Nikita Khrushchev flew in from the steppes of Russia to see for himself this corn granary of the world. The shapely golden ear and graceful stalk also have helped form the state's aesthetic. Declares historian Neil R. Pierce: "There are few more beautiful sights in America than Iowa's farmlands in early autumn, the glistening fields of eight- and ten-foot-high hybrid corn, delicately tasseled, billowing in the wind…" ✱

*Corn Palace, Sioux City,* 1890. The exposition palace is a species of true native architecture from the late 1800s. Palaces were decorated with corn, grass, or coal, according to the theme. Several were built in Sioux City, the first inspired by a bumper corn crop in 1887 and designed by E. W. Loft. This later example was fantastically Moorish, with great arched entrances surmounted by panels wrought in colored corn. A corn-thatched roof made a solid mass of green. *Sioux City Public Museum*

## The Sacred Stalk

Corn is by far the oldest cultivated plant, probably originating in Guatemala. In all history, no corn has been found growing wild; without cultivation, the plant would disappear. The Iowa and other Siouan tribes held red corn sacred, sometimes placing kernels of red corn among their seed corn to ensure fertilization. Columbus, the first European to see corn, named it *maize,* his best guess at the Indian word, but others just applied the Anglo-Saxon word for all small grains: *korn.* In modern times, a near-sacred Iowa ritual has been the corn-husking contest, judged on both speed and accuracy. The winner in a national contest, held in Ankeny since 1922, is decided based on how much weight he can harvest in an hour and 20 minutes; competitors are penalized for ears left behind.

Mush is rough
Mush is tough
Thank thee, Lord,
We've got enough.

*Iowa frontier grace*

### *The Iowa Corn Song*

The land of our pride is old "I - O - WAY"
Prosperous, glorious "I - O - WAY"
Beauteous, bountious "I - O - WAY"
That's where the tall corn grows!…

Although you may come from the East or West
The North or the South you may love the best
The land that is grander than all the rest
That's where the tall corn grows!

*Words and Melody by John O. Knutson*

*That's where the tall corn grows*

Panels from Lowell Houser's *Evolution of Corn* for the Ames Post Office, one of many New Deal mural projects created in Iowa in the late 1930s. Houser depicts the role corn has played from the Mayans to modern times, illustrating Daniel Webster's adage, "Where tillage begins, other arts follow." *Iowa State Historical Society*

**Things to Do**

Iowa's rail and steam-
boat era lives on at:

**Boone & Scenic
Valley Railroad**
Rail trips and historic
exhibits. 800-626-0319

**Mississippi River
Museum**
Exhibits covering 300
years of river history; in
Dubuque. 800-226-3369

**Sergeant Floyd
Riverboat Museum**
Scale steamboat, model
ship-building; in Sioux
City. 712-279-4840

Uniquely situated between two navigable rivers, Iowa depended greatly on these waterways in the early era of settlement. First keelboats and rafts, then paddle-wheel steamers plied up and down the Mississippi and the Missouri, carrying passengers and freight, while steam ferries hauled westward-bound settlers across the rivers. Mail boats kept schedules you could set your watch by.

But commerce also had to move east and west across the state, and before the automobile came to rule, railroads were the means. In 1855, the first bridge across the Mississippi from Illinois was completed, bringing the railroad from Chicago. Only a year later, steamboat and

steam engine literally clashed head-on when the steamer *Effie Afton* rammed and seriously damaged the new bridge—to the cheers of boatmen observing from shore.

After the Civil War, railroad expansion resumed at a feverish pace, and by 1870 Iowa was spanned by four east-west trunk lines. Iowa's link with the Union Pacific, and thus with the West Coast, was finally achieved in 1873, when the first bridge crossed the Missouri at Council Bluffs. ✳

> And I dreamt that a bridge of a single span
> O'er the wide Mississippi was made.
> And I also dreamt like an insane man
> That the railroad there was laid.
>
> *1851 Iowa rhyme*

## "When Iowa goes Democratic, Hell will go Methodist."

*Jonathan Dolliver, U.S. Senator from Iowa, 1884*

**Des Moines Sunday Register**

**ELECTION ANYBODY'S RACE IN IOWA**

America Speaks Poll Predicts F.R. to Win; Literary Digest Gives Majority to Landon

This famous line reflects Iowa's close ties with the Republican Party, founded in 1856 in Iowa City. Disaffected Democrats and Whigs, bolstered by the state's strong Quaker strain, organized a new party that sided with anti-slavery forces and successfully ran Abraham Lincoln for president in 1860. With only brief interludes—the state went for FDR in 1932 and 1936—Iowa has been staunchly Republican ever since, while producing leaders at both ends of the political spectrum.

Agriculture has ever been a potent force in Iowa politics, with farmers tending to vote Republican during affluent times, but swinging around to deliver "protest votes" during periods of hardship. In the Depression years of 1873, 1893, and the early 1930s, important farm reform movements like the Grange and the Farm Holiday Association arose in Iowa. As is fitting for a major farming state, several Iowans have served as Secretary of

Agriculture, the best known being New Dealer Henry Wallace, equally renowned as the inventor of hybrid corn, and "Tama Jim" Wilson, who served under three presidents.

Other prominent Iowa statesmen include Herbert Hoover (the first president from west of the Mississippi), WPA chief Harry Hopkins, 19th-century governors Samuel Kirkwood (who helped found the GOP) and abolitionist James W. Grimes; U.S. Senators Dolliver, Albert Cummins, and William Kenyon, and House Speaker David Henderson. And, in a shining exception to the rule, Democratic Governor Harold E. Hughes was elected in 1962. According to one historian, Hughes was "one of the most charismatic, effective reformers the Plains States have produced." ✱

"IF GOVERNMENT IS SUPPOSED TO BE BASED ON THE will of the people, somebody ought to go and find out what that will is."

*George Gallup, c. 1935*

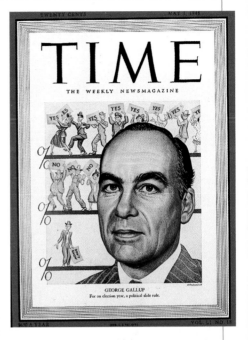

Time magazine named Iowa native and polling pioneer George Gallup its Man of the Year in 1948. © 1948 *Time, Inc. Opposite above:* Front page of the *Des Moines Register* during the 1936 presidential race. *Opposite below:* Cartoon by the *Register's* nationally syndicated Brian Duffy, the latest star in Iowa's tradition of political art. *Courtesy the artist and Des Moines Register*

*"Little towns are mighty big places to be from."*

*Wright Morris,* The Inhabitants

MAIN STREET
I O W A

Many Iowa towns have joined the "Main Street" program, launched in the 1970s by the National Trust for Historic Preservation to revitalize downtowns; the program's logo appears at right.

Iowa's true character lies in its small towns, where most Iowans still live. Of 900 "cities and villages" in the state, just 70 have populations over 5,000. Starting in the 1840s, Iowa was surveyed and plotted into townships and sections, laying down a regular pattern that is strikingly visible from the air. Within this larger scheme, towns were laid out in rectangular grids and lots, with a central village green or town square surrounded by principal streets. Along Iowa's main streets, rows of storefronts built on a regular, human scale provided a sense of unity and balance, with room for individual expression in architectural details and signage.

"ONE OF THE MOST PLEASANT MEN WE MET [in Prairie City] was E. B. Tilden, dealer in fancy groceries, canned goods, fruits, nuts, fine cigars, tobacco, etc. Also runs a very fine ice cream parlor; and the only soda fountain in the place. A better place to refresh oneself is hard to find."

*Story in the* Iowa State Leader, *1880*

*Left:* Civil War veterans march in Boone's Independence Day parade, 1905. *Iowa State Historical Society. Opposite below:* The Wilton Candy Kitchen in Muscatine County has been run by the same family since 1910. *Photo Mike Whye*

Main Street was a magnet for the surrounding farms. Town was where people gathered to buy provisions, go to church and school, attend town meetings, band concerts, and dances, vote, exchange gossip, catch the train, get equipment repaired, march in parades, drink a soda, and so on. Such rituals nurtured the deep roots of Iowa community life. ✿

*Left and above:* Postcard and board game of Iowa's Lincoln Highway, billed as the "Main Street of America." *Lyell Henry and Mount Mercy College*

### In Madison County

**Chamber of Commerce**
Call for maps to the
covered bridges.
800-298-6119

**Francesca's House**
515-981-5268

**John Wayne
Birthplace**
515-462-1044

Madison County is home to some of Iowa's proudest traditions and unique in its concentration of historic covered bridges. The famed bridges are a focal point of the Robert James Waller novel and the movie based on it. Shooting for the film took place in Winterset, the birthplace of another Hollywood great, John Wayne. Six of the original 19 bridges remain. They were covered to preserve the large flooring timbers, more expensive to replace than the roof and sides. (Most of the building was done by local farmers, as payment of their poll tax.) Madison County

Clint Eastwood as Robert Kincaid in the 1995 film *The Bridges of Madison County.* Right: National Geographic provided a mock cover as a prop for the film. *National Geographic Society; photos Ken Regan/Camera Five*

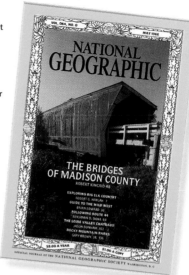

*I ask myself over and over, "What happened to me in Madison County, Iowa?"*

Robert Kincaid, in
The Bridges of Madison County,
by Robert James Waller, 1992

also boasts the hometown of botanist George Washington Carver, the African-American agricultural innovator, and the site where the first Delicious apple was grown. A new tradition is visiting "Francesca's House," the 1880s Winterset homestead that portrayed the heroine's farm in the movie. ❁

*Opposite and left:* Hogback Covered Bridge, built by Benton Jones in 1884, just north of Winterset, is 96 feet long. *Photo Ric MacRae.* Left: Interior framework of Hogback Bridge. *Photo Madison County Chamber of Commerce*

The Des Moines Art Center, originally designed by Eliel Saarinen in 1944, now includes a gallery by I. M. Pei and this new wing by Richard Meier, 1985. *Des Moines Art Center. Below:* Hanging spiral staircase in the rotunda of the Old Stone Capitol in Iowa City, designed by John Francis Rague. *Photo Mike Whye*

Iowa's noteworthy edifices span the range of American architectural styles. The Old Stone Capitol, built in Iowa City in 1842, is a fine example of Greek Revival; it became a museum after the government relocated to Des Moines. The present beauxarts capitol (see *Stately Symbols*) was designed by A. H. Piquenard. Completed in 1884, this splendid domed building has an air of grace and lightness despite its bulk. Another gem is the Grandview Music Pavilion in Sioux City. Designed by Iowa architect Henry Kamphoefer, it was submitted to the Society of Beaux Arts for its Paris prize.

Fine buildings in the Italian Renaissance style are found at the University of Iowa at Iowa City, and Iowa State University at Ames boasts worthy examples of Gothic Revival. Several important churches and the New Melleray Abbey, near Dubuque, embody the Victorian Gothic type. Here and there in Iowa are buildings in the Prairie style developed by Frank Lloyd Wright and Louis Sullivan, and Sioux City's Woodbury County Courthouse, by W. L. Steele, recalls the eclectic, highly embellished urban buildings of Wright and Sullivan. True examples of modernism are rare but include the new Des Moines Arts Center, designed by an international team of architects.

Iowa sculptors won recognition earlier than its painters, and good examples of public sculpture and monuments are scattered around the state. Among the best known are Christian Peterson's terra-cotta murals at Iowa State College. ✹

Terrace Hill, the home of Iowa's governor, is an elaborately detailed Second Empire Victorian mansion built in 1869 for Iowa's first millionaire, Benjamin F. Allen. *Left:* Native American sculptor Allen Houser (1914–1994) created this contemporary statue titled *Prayer of Peace. Muscatine Art Center. Photos Mike Whye*

The home of Milo and Sally Lines George in Sac City, one of George Barber's mail-order designs. *Photo Le Spearman. Below:* Sod houses like this example in West Bend were the commonest kind of dwelling for settlers on the prairie, where wood was relatively scarce. *Photo Ric MacRae*

The first dwellings in Iowa were the earth-covered lodges of prehistoric peoples; later woodland tribes lived in wickiups made of woven reed mats on wood frames, and prairie tribes in tepees. Early settlers made use of the same materials—logs, sod, clay, bark, and mats. The typical pioneer home was a log cabin; as settlement moved north and west, cabins were replaced by buildings of lumber, brick, and stone. Many resembled homes built by the Amana Colony from 1855 to 1870: plain gabled rectangles softened by low-pitched roofs and trellises. Farmhouses were usually boxlike, two-story wood structures, often painted white with rambling additions to house families and help. Later in the 19th century, newly affluent Iowans wanted grand houses, so manors and gingerbread palaces arose in towns from Keokuk to Council Bluffs, blending popular Victorian styles such as Queen Anne, Romanesque, and Colonial Renaissance. Some 200 of them came from the mail-order blueprints of architect George Barber, who sent his designs around the country from Knoxville, Tennessee. ❋

*Above:* The Brucemore home, a modified Queen Anne Victorian in Cedar Rapids. *Photo Mike Whye. Left and below:* Mamie Doud Eisenhower, wife of President Eisenhower, and the interior of her birthplace in Boone, now a visitor attraction. *Photos Mamie Doud Eisenhower Birthplace Home*

**A**rtful objects for everyday use are a feature of most Iowans' lives. The state's folk art traditions derive chiefly from the immigrants that settled there. Groups of French, German, English, Irish, Norwegians, and Swedes emigrated to the state from the 1840s on; Hungarians, Danes, and Czechs followed. Old customs endure in the Bohemian community centered around Cedar Rapids, and among the Dutch living in Pella and its surrounding farms. Germans, perhaps the largest contingent, found homes in many parts of Iowa and still maintain well-defined communities in some. Two communal groups of German origin, the Amish and the Amana Society, are especially active in preserving traditional lifeways and domestic arts.

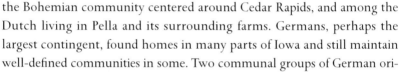

More recently, Iowa has welcomed new immigrant populations of Hispanics and Asians—mainly tribal Laotians—who have settled in western Iowa around Sioux City and Storm Lake, bringing their own lively and colorful celebrations and crafts. ✻

"ONE THING THAT ALL THE BASKETS HAD WAS...A removable bottom rim. The rim would wear, and then you could pull it off and put a new one on."

*Joanna Schanz, Amana basket maker, on Amana baskets*

Left: Norwegian rose-maling, a traditional decorative art of painting on wood. *Photo David Cavagnaro. Below:* Amana tin wedding cake mold by William Metz, 1988. *Photo Steven Ohrn. Opposite above:* Intricately hand-painted wooden eggs are a Czech custom practiced by Iowa's Bohemian immigrants. *Opposite below:* Amana "Apple Picker" basket (date unknown) of peeled cultivated willow. *Photos Steven Ohrn*

"SCRATCH ANY IOWAN AND YOU'LL FIND SOMEONE WHO NOT only knows how to cope, but often copes with a sense of flair, eccentricity, or inventiveness....Open the door to an Iowa home, and inside you may still find a crazy quilt in a frame, pieces of an old pair of brown coveralls and a red stocking cap sewn together to make a beautiful new creation."

*Mary Swander*

"THAT STAR MOLD WAS ONLY USED FOR marble cake. If someone used it for another cake, people didn't think it tasted as good."

*Lisette Metz*

Amana lace doily by an unknown artist, c. 1980s. *Photo Steven Ohrn. Below:* Seven-foot basswood clock depicting the Fairfield Gas Engine, carved by artist John McLain, 1977. *Photo Le Spearman Opposite above:* Four-patch cotton quilt top by an unknown quilter (possibly a young girl named Marg), c. 1875–1910. *Iowa State Historical Society. Opposite below:* Male wood duck, carved and painted by Lyle Roberts, c. 1981. *Photo Steven Ohrn*

"WOMEN CROCHETED PRETTY THINGS. They considered them practical because they'd cover a table with a doily. It was *Zeitvertreib*—pastime or amusement."

*Elizabeth Schoenfelder*

## The Amana Aesthetic

The Community of True Inspiration arose in Germany in the early 18th century and, under visionary leader Christian Metz, evolved along communal lines. Forced out of Germany by ongoing persecution, they settled first in upstate New York and in 1855 relocated to east central Iowa, calling themselves the Amana Society (the word means "remain true"). Today, the Amana Colonies comprise five villages and many farms scattered through 26,000 acres of gentle hills and valleys. Unlike the Amish, the Amanans have adapted to modern life, founding woolen mills and furniture and appliance manufactures. Yet they retain their spiritual heritage and their aesthetic of simple, functional, beautifully crafted objects such as baskets, throw rugs, quilts and other textiles, woodwork, and tinware. The culture of old Amana is nurtured and protected by an arts guild.

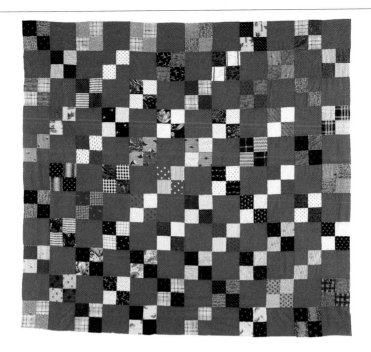

"IT WAS THE FAMILY CUSTOM TO GATHER AROUND THE FIRE
on winter evenings....One of the girls would read aloud
while the others would knit or sew, 'resting work,' they
called it. Remembering the yards of stitching and knit-
ting, all the garments that were fashioned by hand,
we could understand Susan's impatience with those
who were content to sit with 'idle hands.'"

*Grace Bouler Forgrave, "Fragrant Hearts,"*
*a reminiscence about Iowa life from the 1840s to 1860s*

## "If you build it, he will come."

*From the movie* Field of Dreams

**O**ur "national pastime" has thrived in Iowa's fields and small towns almost since baseball's beginnings. More than 100 major leaguers have hailed from the state, including some great stars like fastball pitcher Bob Feller and, in the old days, Cap Anson, the great first baseman for the Chicago White Stockings of 1876 to 1897. One of Cap's teammates was outfielder Billy Sunday, whose throw, Anson complained, "landed in the hands like a chunk of lead." Sunday, who later became a hellfire Evangelist preacher, once prayed as he chased down a towering line drive: "God, if you ever helped mortal man, help me to get that ball, and you haven't very much time to

Iowa's Cap Anson in his Chicago White Stockings uniform. *Iowa Historical Society. Right:* They're still coming to the ballfield built for *Field of Dreams,* where pick-up games regularly take place. *Photo Mike Whye. Opposite:* Cover illustration by Wendell Minor for *The Iowa Baseball Confederacy* by W. P. Kinsella, 1986. *Courtesy Wendell Minor*

## Iowa's Baseball Hall of Fame

Calvin McVey
Montrose

Fred Clarke
Des Moines

Edmund "Bing" Miller
Vinton

Billy Sunday
Ames

Adrian C. "Cap" Anson
Marshalltown

Hal Trosky
Norway

Urban "Red" Faber
Dubuque

Dave "Beauty" Bancroft
Sioux City

Bob Feller
Van Meter

Dazzy Vance
Orient

Mace Brown
North English

George Pipgrass
Denison

make up your mind, either." God's response is not recorded, but supernatural events *may* take place from time to time on Iowa's diamonds—at least, if the movies are to be believed. ✻

ART OF THE STATE 69

Rogers & Hammerstein set *State Fair* to music in a 1945 Technicolor movie starring Jean Crain and Dana Andrews, shown in this poster. *Photofest photo.* Opposite above: Apple pie with crust decorations, baked according to official State Fair rules. *Photo (and pie) Le Spearman.* Opposite below: Great Colonel, a prize-winning Duroc boar from Creston, at a circa 1920s Iowa State Fair. *Wallaces' Farmer*

The granddaddy of them all, Iowa's State Fair is an annual rite that dates nearly from the founding of the state—1997 marked its 139th observation. Hundreds of thousands of Iowans and visitors converge on the Des Moines fairgrounds site for nearly two weeks at summer's end to take part in this extravaganza of farm culture, featuring some 160 activities on 400 acres. (The entire district is listed on National Register of Historic Places.) The line-up includes big-name entertainment, grandstand events like horse shows and racing, thrills and chills on the midway, the Iowa Art Salon, agricultural and industrial exhibits, and of course, livestock and food contests. Four-H youngsters show off their prize animals, and at the fair's close, a "Million Dollar Stock Parade" of beribboned winners passes before the grandstand. ✱

## An Iowa Classic

In 1932, the fourth-generation Iowa writer Phil Stong published his novel *State Fair* to instant acclaim. This good-humored portrait of Iowa's classic ritual stars the Frake family—Abel and wife Melissa, son Wayne, and daughter Margy— who descend on the fair with their prize hog Blue Boy and Melissa's homemade pickles, in hopes of prizes and romance. The tale has been dramatized many times, beginning with a 1935 black-and-white (nonmusical) film starring Will Rogers, but it wasn't until 1995 that a full-fledged theatrical production hit the boards. It opened, appropriately, in Des Moines, with the governor presiding, and a successful Broadway run followed.

*The Storekeeper, a gloomy Greek chorus of a character, believes that "Heaven ordains all things for the worse." He warns Abel Frake:* "Don't let your hog get too good. Because he's the best hog…he'll never win the sweepstakes. If a hog or man ever got what he was entitled to once, the eternal stars would quit making melody in the spheres."

*Phil Stong,* State Fair, *1932*

Grant Wood's *Self-Portrait, 1932–41,* shows the artist regarding the world warily; a windmill proclaims his allegiance to the farming landscape. *Davenport Museum of Art. Opposite:* The landmark *American Gothic* of 1930 has become a much-beloved and parodied icon. *The Art Institute of Chicago. Both © Est. Grant Wood/VAGA, NY*

One of America's distinguished painters and a leading Regionalist, Grant Wood was born in 1892 in Anamosa. The son of Quaker farmers, he absorbed from his neighbors the qualities of honesty and patient craftmanship that came to characterize his work. As a young man he worked in metal and jewelry, and taught art in the Cedar Rapids public schools. In 1920 Wood left home to stretch his artistic wings in Paris, but soon wearied of the Continent and his experiments in Impressionism. It was then he realized "that all the really good ideas I'd ever had came to me while I was milking a cow." His return

to America coincided with a rising national urge, in the 1920s and 30s, to nurture and promote homegrown culture. Wood's now-famous *American Gothic* created a stir when shown at Chicago's Art Institute in 1930, and his scenes of Iowa rural life began appearing at galleries there and in New York. His paintings elevate the commonplace subject of fields and farmers into clean-edged American icons; they lift the spirit and remind us of our heartland roots. ✱

*Dinner for Threshers*, 1934. Wood's celebration of community and social ritual among Iowa farmers took its formal composition from a Renaissance triptych. *Fine Arts Museums of San Francisco, Gift of Mr. and Mrs. John D. Rockefeller III, 1979.7.105*

*Portrait of Nan*, 1933. Wood's younger sister Nan was his model on several occasions; it is her face "drawn out long" on the farm wife in his famous *American Gothic*. *Elvehjem Museum of Art.* © *Estate of Grant Wood/ VAGA, NY*

*Arbor Day*, 1932, is another of Wood's depictions of frontier ritual, a scene from the 1890s. By Wood's day, the trees planted then would have sheltered the schoolhouse. *Cedar Rapids, Iowa, Community School District. © Estate of Grant Wood/VAGA, NY*

CHAUTAUQUA
SPRINGVILLE     JUNE 25-30

1915

SIX BIG       TWELVE
DAYS          PROGRAMS

JONES CHAUTAUQUA SYSTEM
THE WORLDS GREATEST
CHAUTAUQUA SYSTEM

The Chautauqua tours, usually performed in large tents, gave many Iowans their only experience of spoken theater and other "serious" entertainment. *Above:* A 1915 Chautauqua program. *Right:* Popular literature thrived in the late 1800s in the form of the dime novel, and Iowa produced one of its chief perpetrators, Oliver "Oll" Combs. Shown is a cover for *Old Bald Head. Iowa State Historical Society*

Literature and drama have thrived on Iowa soil since the days of Chief Black Hawk's eloquent oratory. Pioneer diaries and letters became source material for historians and novelists. Late in the last century, America's growing ambitions encouraged the growth of native writing in Iowa, as well as performance tours and tent shows like the Lyceum and Chautauqua movements. Nearly every small town built its own "opera house"—most often used not for opera but for traveling theatricals and community events.

The early to middle 1900s saw the rise of literary regionalism, with gritty portrayals of Iowa rural life by writers like Hamlin Garland, Herbert Quick, and Ruth Suckow. A turn-of-the-century literary enclave in Davenport included George Cram Cook and his wife, playwright Susan Glaspell, who helped nurture American drama. They went on to found in 1913 the Provincetown Players, famed for its association with Eugene O'Neill. Contemporary Iowa writers of note include the poets

BEADLE'S
New Dime Novels

Old Bald Head.

Mary Swander, Michael Carey, and Mesquakie writer Ray Young Bear. And two of Jane Smiley's acclaimed novels, *A Thousand Acres* (also a 1997 film) and *Moo,* are set in Iowa's countryside and university towns. ✳

"IOWA HAS NOT ALWAYS SMILED ON HER DREAMERS, HER POETS, her children with the divine fire in their souls, whether much or little of it.... And yet I know if the artist in Iowa could only be allowed such a life of the soul as would impel him to respect his Iowa materials, and to ponder them long enough and deeply enough, every element of great art would be found here."

*Herbert Quick,* The Hawkeye, *1923*

Painted canvas "drops" were the usual form of scenery in the Midwest's early opera houses. This superb town drop was painted by Sosman and Landis of Chicago for the opera house in Oxford Junction, Iowa. Traveling companies chalked the play's title on the blank sign. *Museum of Repertoire Americana*

# "Good poets, like good hybrid corn

Portrait of the young Samuel Clemens by an unknown artist, c. 1859. It hangs in the Keokuk Public Library, where examples of Twain's printing handiwork are also displayed. *Photo Dreasler Photography Right:* Max Beerbohm's cartoon of Oscar Wilde speaking to Iowa farmers on his 1882 tour of America. The Sioux City *Journal* wrote, "If art is responsible for the like of him, we want no art in ours." *Tate Gallery/ Art Resource*

## Mark Twain in Keokuk

Samuel Clemens came upriver to Keokuk in 1855, where he stayed two years, working in the printing shop of his brother, Orion. Sam set most of the type for Keokuk's *First Directory,* in which he listed himself as an "antiquarian"—just because he felt every town should have one. Clemens published his first written piece, the "Snodgrass Letters," in the *Keokuk Post.* He left town for several reasons, but claimed it was because he'd found $50 on the street and couldn't bear the thought that its owner might respond to his advertisement and claim it. "I felt I must take that money out of danger, so I bought a ticket to Cincinnati...."

"WHATEVER REAL VALUE THE CULTURE AND ART OF IOWA CAN have is founded upon this bedrock [the working farmers]....
Our varying nationalities meet in this rich soil which has still some of the old pioneer virtue of sturdy freshness—perhaps the only virtue, genuine and clearly distinguishable from all others, which the native culture of this young country has to offer...."

Ruth Suckow, "Iowa," in the
American Mercury, *1926*

*ιre both born and made."*

Paul Engle, founder of the Iowa Writers Workshop

## A Workshop for Words

The Poetry and Fiction Workshops at the University of Iowa in Iowa City have long been a fertile seedbed for literary talent. One of the nation's first academic programs for creative writing, it was established in the early 1940s by Iowa poet Paul Engle and several associates. Its distinguished faculty and roster of visiting writers have included John Berryman, Donald Justice, Philip Roth, Kurt Vonnegut, Nelson Algren, Robert Creeley, Joyce Carol Oates, Herbert Gold, and current director Frank Conroy. In the 1960s the program added an International Workshop with participants from around the globe. Notable workshop graduates include Wallace Stegner, Flannery O'Connor, and Philip Levine.

Paul Engle as a young man. Poet and teacher Paul Engle was born in Cedar Rapids. After study abroad he took a post at the university in 1937, where he formed the connections that led to creating the writer's workshop, which he directed from 1941 to 1966. *Photo courtesy Connie Brothers*

The Czech composer Antonín Dvořák spent the summer of 1893 in Spillville, an Iowa town with strong Bohemian roots. There he worked on his famous Ninth Symphony, the "New World." *Below:* A woodcut portrait of the composer and a few bars from the score of the "New World." *Opposite:* Professor Harold Hill, played by Robert Preston, leads the children of River City in the big number "Seventy-Six Trombones" from the Tony-winning Best Musical of 1958, *The Music Man. Photofest photo*

Iowa's music is composed of many strains. Native Iowans echoed birdsong and other sounds from nature on drums, rattles, whistles, and red cedar flutes. European settlers brought their music along: German, Czech, and Welsh immigrants formed bands, choral groups, and accordion ensembles. More than most states, Iowa fostered music in its rural areas; the Thursday night "singing school" was a ritual for young people. And there are strong traditions of hymn writing and folk music; ethnic music festivals are especially popular in the southwest. But brass bands are Iowa's musical claim to fame. Funded by an Iowa Band Law, towns built bandstands and supported ensembles. The March King himself, John Philip Sousa, was once lured to Iowa to play a few concerts. Circus composer Karl King hailed from Fort Dodge, and the "Music Man," Meredith Willson, turned his band-focused childhood in Mason City ("River City") into one of America's best-loved musicals. ✱

### *"Iowa Stubborn"*

*from* The Music Man
*Music and Lyrics by Meredith Willson*

Oh, there's nothing halfway about
the Iowa way we treat you,
When we treat you, which we may
    not do at all.
There's an Iowa kinda special
chip-on-the-shoulder attitude
We've never been without that we recall.
We can be cold as our falling thermometer
    in December,
if you ask about our weather in July.

And we're so by God stubborn we can
stand touching noses for a week at a time
and never see eye to eye. . . .
But we'll give you our shirt, and a
    back to go with it,
if your crop should happen to die.
So what the heck! You're welcome.
Glad to have you with us,
Even though we may not ever mention it again.
You really ought to give Iowa a try!

### Things to Do

Iowa is a great place for music festivals: jazz, brass bands, bluegrass, you name it. To name just a few:

**The Glenn Miller Festival**
Clarinda
Annually in June

**The North Iowa Band Festival**
Mason City
Annually in June

**Bix Beiderbecke Memorial Festival**
Davenport
Annually in July

### *Muziky, Muziky*

Muziky, muziky,
vy pekne hrajete;
vy jste mne ze spaní,
probudily.

Ja jsem se nevyspal,
holku jsem nedostal;
tím jste vy muziky,
samy vinny.

### *Dance Band, Dance Band*

Dance band, dance band,
You are playing very well;
From a nice sleep,
You woke me up.

I didn't sleep enough,
I didn't get the girl;
And music band,
That's your own fault.

*Words to a traditional Czech song, as played by the accordion bands of east-central Iowa*

## Glenn, Bix, and Buddy

Popular music in Iowa, like the rest of America, wouldn't exist without the influence of African-American sounds. By the 1850s, showboats were already steaming into Iowa's river towns, bringing minstrel shows into Iowa's river towns. Half a century later, the strains of ragtime and blues came floating up the Mississippi to take root in Iowa soil. One of those river towns was Davenport, where in 1903 the brilliant cornetist Leon Bismark ("Bix") Beiderbecke was born. Just a year later, Alton Glenn Miller was born near Clarinda; he too grew up to be one of the nation's greatest jazzmen. A Midwestern boy of a later generation, pioneering rock 'n' roller Buddy Holly, gave his last concert in the Surf Ballroom at Clear Lake.

Alton Glenn Miller. The Glenn Miller Birthplace Society in Clarinda sponsors an annual festival. *Glenn Miller Birthplace Society. Below:* The Keota Ladies' Band, c. 1911–12. Brass bands evolved from military fife-and-drum corps. *Iowa State Historical Society. Opposite:* The Metro Opera Company of Des Moines, which celebrated its 25th anniversary in 1997, draws visitors from all over the Midwest. *Photo John F. Schultz*

"I TOLD BIX TO JUST PLAY AND HE'D PLEASE THE CATS. BUT YOU take a genius and he's never satisfied....If that boy had lived, he'd been the greatest."

*Louis Armstrong*

Contemporary art is alive and well in Iowa. In this age of mobility and quick communication, being isolated from the country's leading art centers seems untroubling to serious artists, who migrate here from many other states as well as from abroad. The best of current Iowa fine art is on display annually in the juried exhibit "Iowa Artists," mounted by the Des Moines Art Center. This show, and others statewide, reveals that Iowa artists share the concerns of artists everywhere, and work in the wide range of media typical of our time. Their work, says one curator, shows "influences ranging from the Chicago Imagist painters,

to the cool, intellectual modernism of the younger East Coast generation, to the rich legacy of Iowa university printmakers and photographers." Not all deal in subjects specific to the state; many find their own variations on the modernist themes of Cubism, Surrealism, and Dada. But some do document or comment on local events. Others celebrate the land uncritically, or interpret landscape in ways unthought of by earlier generations; environmental concerns emerge strongly. A few aim to show darker sides of Iowa's rural culture (as did Iowa fiction much earlier). Along with Iowa's current crop of writers, musicians, architects, and others, the state's visual artists are looking forward, yet keeping an eye on a past worth remembering. ✻

*Above: Reclamation of a Small Waste Area by Will Mentor, oil on wood, 1996. Opposite above: Midway by Victor McCullough, 1994, was named Best of Show at the 1994 "Iowa Artists" Exhibit. Opposite below: Marvin's Barn by Martha Yoder, intaglio, 1996. All, courtesy of the artist*

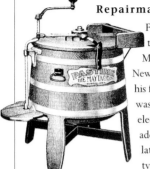

### Repairman Wanted

Fred Maytag, the "Washing Machine King" of Newton, introduced his first commercial washer in 1907. An electric motor was added two years later. The prototype washer is on display at the Jasper County Historical Museum in Newton.

### Hot Air Heaven

Indianola, in south-central Iowa, is home to the National Balloon Museum. A well-designed contemporary building houses a

collection of ballooning artifacts and memorabilia depicting the history of hot-air and gas ballooning. Balloons regularly make ascensions from the surrounding countryside.

### Little Churches

Near Festina stands the world's smallest church, the St. Anthony of Padua Chapel, which seats just eight in its 14-by-20-foot interior. Located on the former site of a log-cabin mission from the 1840s, it was rebuilt in its present form in 1885. Nashua is home to the "Little Brown Church in the Vale," as described in the nostalgic

song by William S. Pitts ("Oh, come to the church in the wildwood. . . ."). A magnet for couples, it hosts more than 800 weddings every year.

### Czech Out the Clocks

In Spillville, the Bily Clock Museum displays elaborate timepieces hand-carved by Joseph and Frank Bily over 30 years. Upstairs, in the Antonín Dvořák Exhibit, are memorabilia of the Czech composer's visit to this Bohemian community in the summer of 1893.

### Grotto of the Redemption

Located in West Bend is the world's largest grotto, sometimes called the "Eighth Wonder of the World." A composite of nine separate grottos portrays the life of Christ in stones and gems—the largest collection of minerals and petrification concentrated in any one spot worldwide. Father Paul Dobberstein started building the Grotto in 1912; when he died 42 years later, it covered an entire city block.

### A Lotta Java

Rising nearly 125 feet above the mainly Scandinavian community of Stanton is the brightly painted Swedish Coffeepot—world's largest coffeepot. A symbol of the town's hospitality, it holds 40,000 gallons (that's 640,000 cups of java). Stanton is also home to "Mrs. Olson," TV's long-lasting, lilting-voiced coffee pitchwoman.

### The "Keebler Tree"

A storm blew off the top of a tree on Jerry Allen's farm in southeastern Iowa. Allen, an electrical engineer, added a peaked roof, outside stairway, and door to the hollow trunk, creating a perfect "elf house" (and a great example of everyday Iowa ingenuity). Elves over 2 feet tall need not apply.

# Great People

*A selective listing of native Iowans, concentrating on the arts.*

**Leon Bismarck (Bix) Beiderbecke** (1903–1931), jazz cornetist and composer

**Fran Allison** (1907–1989), TV puppeteer of "Kukla, Fran and Ollie" fame

**Black Hawk** (1767–1838), Sauk Indian chief

**Amelia Jenkins Bloomer** (1818–1894), social and sartorial reformer

**Johnny Carson** (b. 1925), talk show host

**Carrie Chapman Catt** (1859–1947), educator and suffragist leader

**William Frederick "Buffalo Bill" Cody** (1846–1917), frontiersman and showman

**Mamie Doud Eisenhower** (1890–1969), First Lady

**William Frawley** (1887–1966), actor, Fred in "I Love Lucy"

**George Gallup** (1901–1984), public-opinion expert

**Hamlin Garland** (1860–1940), novelist of pioneer life

**Susan Glaspell** (1882–1948), playwright, Pulitzer Prize winner in drama

**Herbert Hoover** (1874–1964), geologist, engineer, 31st U.S. president

**Mackinlay Kantor** (1904–1977), author, Pulitzer Prize winner in fiction

**Ann Landers** (b. 1918), advice columnist

**Aldo Leopold** (1886–1948), ecologist

**Jerry Mathers** (b. 1948), actor, Beaver Cleaver on "Leave It to Beaver"

**Glenn Miller** (1904–1944), jazz trombonist, big-band leader

**Herbert Quick** (1861–1925), novelist of rural Iowa

**Harry Reasoner** (1923–1991), television journalist

**Donna Reed** (1921–1986), actress, star of "The Donna Reed Show"

**Alfred, Charles, and John Ringling,** circus impresarios

**Lillian Russell** (1861–1922), singer and comedienne

**Wallace Stegner** (1909–1993), novelist and essayist

**Ruck Suckow** (1892–1960), novelist of farm life

**James Alfred Van Allen** (b. 1914), physicist, discovered cosmic rays

**John Wayne** (1907–1979), actor and American icon

**Meredith Willson** (1902–1984), Broadway composer and lyricist

**Grant Wood** (1892–1942), Regionalist painter

## . . . and Great Places

*Some interesting derivations of Iowa place names.*

**Anamosa** Meaning "white fawn," the name of a Winnebago chief's daughter. In love with a white man, legend says, she leaped to her death into a river rather than marry her father's choice.

**Britt** Site of a famous hoax perpetrated by journalist "Bailey of Britt," who announced a national hobo convention there. The joke later became a reality.

**California** Earlier called Yazoo, it was renamed in the expectation that California-bound passengers would change trains at this junction.

**Council Bluffs** On the bluffs above the Missouri, a rendezvous for Indians and traders.

**Des Moines** After the Des Moines River, which French explorers called "de Moyen" or the "middle" river, between the Mississippi and the Missouri.

**Dubuque** For Julian Dubuque, the enterprising French trader who persuaded the Fox tribe to let him work nearby lead mines.

**Elkader** Named for an Algerian chieftain, Abd-el-Kader, who defended his land from French imperialism.

**Guttenberg** Originally called Prairie La Porte, the town was renamed in honor of the printer Gutenberg, but misspelled in a typographical error!

**Keokuk** City on the Mississippi, one of several place names honoring this Sauk chief.

**Mason City** Originally known as Masonic Grove; freemasonry has long been a strong element in Iowa.

**Ottumwa** On the Des Moines River; from an Indian word meaning "rippling waters."

**Primghar** An anagram of the names of eight early settlers.

**Schleswig** For the inhabitants' home province in Prussia.

**Spirit Lake** On an island in this lake lived demonic spirits, according to Indian legend, which devoured all who attempted to land on it.

**What Cheer** Named by a Rhode Islander: founder Roger Williams greeted the Indians in that colony with the phrase.

**Winterset** "Summerset" was first proposed for this town, but one resident, shivering and in his cups, declared, "You'd a damn sight better name it Winterset!"

**Zwingle** For Ulrich Zwingli, a 19th-century Swiss Protestant reformer.

And just for fun: **Jollyville**.

**Lamoni** Above, the home of Joseph Smith in this town named for a "righteous king" from the Book of Mormon.

# IOWA BY THE SEASONS
## A Perennial Calendar of Events and Festivals

*Here is a selective listing of events that take place each year in the months noted;
we suggest calling ahead to local chambers of commerce for dates and details.*

## January

Allamakee County
*Allamakee County Winterfest and Sportsman's Club Fisheree*
Ice fishing and winter sports.

Cherokee
*Off-Shore Masters Golf Tournament*
Golfing on a frozen lake.

Clear Lake
*Buddy Holly Festival*

Clinton
*Annual Bald Eagle Watch*
Outdoor viewing of bald eagles at Lock and Dam 13; similar events in Dubuque and elsewhere.

Des Moines
*Breath of Spring Floral Show*
*Festival of Lanterns: Botanical Center*

Monticello
*Winter Carnival*
Snow-sculpting, rides, games.

## February

Cedar Rapids
*Annual Bassmasters Ice Fisheree*
*Country Folk Art Show*

Charles City
*Winter Wonderland Festival*
Great chili cook-off, fireworks, and parade.

Dubuque
*Iowa Winter Games*

## March

Cedar Falls
*Maple Syrup Festival*
The making of maple syrup at the Hartman Sugarbush.

Cedar Rapids
*Maple Syrup Festival*
Maple syrup demonstrations at Indian Creek Nature Center.

*Czech and Slovak Easter Traditions*
Demonstrations of traditional Easter arts and crafts.

Mason City
*Spring Craft Show*

Sioux City
*Siouxland Multicultural Ethnic Fair*

## April

Bellevue
*Bellevue Mermaid Watch*
Arrival of mermaids from the Mississippi River signals the beginning of spring.

Cedar Rapids
*Cedar Rapids Antique Show and Collector's Fair*

Des Moines
*Summer Sunshine Floral Show: Botanical Center*

Kalona
*Kalona Quilt Show and Sale*
Quilts from the Amish country.

Sioux City
*Tough Man/Tough Woman Contest*

## May

Cedar Rapids
*Houby Days: Czech Village*
Two-day celebration of the houby (Czech for mushroom).

*Ushers Ferry Antique Engine Show*
Exhibition of gas and steam engines and vintage cars.

Des Moines
*Salisbury House May Festival*
Revival of Renaissance times and traditions.

Dubuque
*Dubuquefest*
Iowa's largest all-arts festival.

Elk Horn
*Tivoli Festival*
Danish celebration with parade, dancers, and Danish foods.

Mason City
*North Iowa Band Festival*
Rhythm and brass band music.

*North Iowa Bluegrass Festival*

New London
*Redbud Festival*
Hundreds of redbud trees in bloom.

Pella
*Pella Tulip Time Festival*

Stanhope
*Kite Fly*
Demonstrations by amateur and
professional kite enthusiasts.

## June

Burlington
*Burlington Steamboat Days/
American Music Festival*

Clarinda
*Glenn Miller Festival*

Denison
*Donna Reed Festival for the
Performing Arts*

Hopkinton
*Civil War Days*
Oldest Civil War event in Iowa.

Indianola
*Des Moines Metro Opera
Summer Season*

Iowa City
*Iowa Arts Festival*

Macksburg
*National Skillet Throw Contest*

Stone City–Anamosa
*Grant Wood Art Festival*

## July

Across the state
*RAGBRAI: Register's Annual
Great Bike Ride Across Iowa*

Davenport
*Bix Beiderbecke Memorial
Jazz Festival*

Decorah
*Nordic Festival*
Scandinavian food, music,
dance, and folk art.

Sac City
*Chautauqua Days*
Re-enactment of Chautauqua
shows; games and fireworks.

## August

Avoca
*Old-Time Country Music Contest,
Festival, and Pioneer Exposition*

Britt
*National Hobo Convention*
Begun as a hoax, this annual event
crowns a hobo king and queen.

Des Moines
*Iowa State Fair*

Dubuque
*Dragon Boat Festival*
Chinese dragon boats race on
the Mississippi.

Mount Pleasant
*Midwest Old Threshers Reunion*
Agricultural exhibits from the
days of steam power.

Nevada
*Lincoln Highway Days*
Community celebration of
Iowa's famous road.

Storm Lake
*Great Iowa Balloon Race*
Hot-air balloon contest over
Storm Lake.

Tama
*Meskwaki Powwow*
Celebration of Meskwaki
traditions, food, and dance.

## September

Fort Madison
*Fort Madison Tri-State Rodeo*

Drakesville
*Drakesville Music Reunion*
Country, bluegrass, and old-
time music.

Spencer
*Clay County Fair*
"World's greatest county fair."

Woodbine
*Western Iowa Apple Fest*

## October

Amana Villages
*Oktoberfest*
Autumn celebration with polka
music, beer, and bratwurst.

Waverly
*Waverly Midwest Horse Sale*
Prime draft horses attract buyers
from many states.

Winterset
*Madison County Covered Bridge
Festival*
Cross-country tour of bridges.

## November

Dyersville
*Annual National Farm Toy Show*

Elk Horn and Kimballton
*Julefest*
Danish holiday celebration.

## December

Orange County
*Sinterklaas Day*
Celebration of the Dutch
Santa Claus.

Manning
*Weihnachtsfest*
German Christmas celebration.

# WHERE TO GO
## Museums, Attractions, Gardens, and Other Arts Resources

*Call for seasons and hours when open.*

### Museums

BILY CLOCKS MUSEUM/ANTONIN DVORAK EXHIBIT
Main St., Spillville, 319-562-3569
*See clocks designed and hand-carved by Joseph and Frank Bily and visit the Dvorak Exhibit upstairs.*

BRUNNIER ART MUSEUM
290 Scherman Building, Ames, 515-294-3342
*National and international art exhibitions, collections of glass, ceramics, and art from eastern and western cultures.*

BUFFALO BILL MUSEUM
200 N. River Drive, LeClaire, 319-289-5580
*Memorial and tribute to William F. "Buffalo Bill" Cody.*

CEDAR RAPIDS MUSEUM OF ART
410 Third Ave. SE, Cedar Rapids, 319-366-7503
*World's largest collection of Grant Wood pieces; also works by Marvin Cone, Mauricio Lasansky, and Malvina Hoffman.*

DAVENPORT MUSEUM OF ART
1737 W 12th St., Davenport, 319-326-7804
*Haitian art collection, Grant Wood self-portrait, lithographs by Thomas Hart Benton, and other Regionalist works.*

DES MOINES ART CENTER
4700 Grand Ave., Des Moines, 515-277-4405
*Building designed by internationally recognized architects houses a fine permanent collection of 19th- and 20th-century works.*

DUBUQUE MUSEUM OF ART
36 E. Eighth St., Dubuque, 319-557-1851
*Displays works by local and nationally known artists.*

HOBO MUSEUM
51 Main Ave. S., Britt, 515-843-3867
*The "only hobo museum in existence"; pictures and artifacts.*

HOUSE OF DOLLS MUSEUM
2021 10th St., Emmetsburg, 712-852-3368
*Private collection features 10,000 dolls dating from 1865.*

KALONA QUILT AND TEXTILE MUSEUM
515 B Ave., Kalona, 319-656-2240
*Antique quilts and textiles from the 1800s to the mid-1900s.*

CHARLES H. MACNIDER MUSEUM
303 Second St. SE, Mason City, 515-421-3666
*Tudor-style mansion houses American art and the largest collection anywhere of puppets and props by puppeteer Bil Baird.*

MIDWEST OLD THRESHERS HERITAGE MUSEUMS
1887 Threshers Rd., Mount Pleasant, 319-385-8937
*Steam traction engines, antique tractors, and farming exhibits.*

MISSISSIPPI RIVER MUSEUM
Third St. Ice Harbor, Dubuque, 319-557-9545
*Covers 300 years of river history with life-sized exhibits and the sidewheeler William M. Black, a 277-foot dredge boat.*

MUSEUM OF AMANA HISTORY
4310 220 Trail, Amana, 319-622-3567
*Exhibits portray the story of the Amana Colonies.*

MUSEUM OF REPERTOIRE AMERICANA
1887 Threshers Rd., Mount Pleasant, 319-385-9432
*America's largest collection of early tent, folk, and repertoire theater; displays more than 35 painted stage curtains.*

NATIONAL CZECH AND SLOVAK MUSEUM AND LIBRARY
30 16th Ave. SW, Cedar Rapids, 319-362-8500
*Largest collection of Czech and Slovak costumes in the U.S.*

NATIONAL FARM TOY MUSEUM
1110 16th Ave SE, Dyersville, 319-875-2727
*Features farm toys, trucks, and other toys.*

## SIOUX CITY ART CENTER
225 Nebraska St., Sioux City, 712-279-6272
*45,500 square-foot facility with 900-piece art collection emphasizing contemporary Upper Midwest artists.*

## UNIVERSITY OF IOWA MUSEUM OF ART
150 N. Riverside Drive, Iowa City, 319-335-1727
*Permanent collection of more than 9,000 works of art, with collections of African sculpture as its centerpiece.*

## VESTERHEIM NORWEGIAN–AMERICAN MUSEUM
502 W. Walter St., Decorah, 319-382-9681
*One of America's largest museums devoted to an immigrant group: costumes, room settings, folk art, and pioneer homes.*

## Attractions

## CHAUTAUQUA BUILDING
615 W. Main St., Sac City, 712-662-7383
*Built in 1908, the state's only existing Chautauqua building.*

## COUNTRY RELICS VILLAGE
Hwy 17 N, 1.5 miles from Stanhope, 515-826-3491
*Scale village decorated with children's furnishings and toys.*

## DONNA REED CENTER FOR THE PERFORMING ARTS
Broadway and Main Sts., Denison, 712-263-3334
*Houses the Donna Reed Foundation and features personal and movie memorabilia from Donna Reed's life.*

## EFFIGY MOUNDS NATIONAL MONUMENT
151 Hwy. 76, 3 miles north of Marquette, 319-873-3491
*View 200 prehistoric American Indian burial and ceremonial mounds, dating from 500 B.C. to 1300 A.D.*

## FENELON PLACE ELEVATOR COMPANY
512 Fenelon Place, Dubuque, 319-582-6496
*The world's shortest and steepest railway, 296 feet long.*

## "FIELD OF DREAMS" MOVIE SITE
Lansing Road, Dyersville, 319-875-8404

*Located on two farms, the baseball diamond "field" was created in the summer of 1988 for the film.*

## GRANT WOOD TOURISM CENTER AND GALLERY
124 E. Main St., Anamosa, 319-462-4267
*Prints and photos of the original Grant Wood Colony in Stone City; exhibit of "American Gothic" caricatures.*

## HISTORIC SQUIRREL CAGE JAIL
226 Pearl St., Council Bluffs, 712-323-2509
*One of the last remaining examples of the "Lazy Susan" jails, featuring a rotating cage with pie-shaped cells.*

## IOWA STATE FAIRGROUNDS
E. 30th and University Ave., Des Moines, 515-262-3111
*Site of the Iowa State Fair and activities year-round.*

## LITTLE BROWN CHURCH
2730 Cheyenne Ave., Nashua, 515-435-2027
*Visitors welcome anytime to this church made famous by the song "Little Brown Church in the Vale."*

## LIVING HISTORY FARMS
2600 NW 111th St., Urbandale, 515-278-5286
*Five sites depicting the movement of the land from a 1700 Ioway Indian village to a modern crop center.*

## PELLA HISTORICAL VILLAGE
507 Franklin St., Pella, 515-628-4311
*Tour 21 buildings, some over 100 years old, including a house, gristmill, bakery, and miniature Dutch Village.*

## STORY CITY ANTIQUE CAROUSEL
North Park, Story City, 515-733-4214
*Restored 1913 Hershel-Spillman carousel features hand-carved wooden animals and a 1936 Wurlitzer band organ.*

## SURF BALLROOM
460 N. Shore Dr., Clear Lake, 515-357-6151
*Historic ballroom where big bands played and singer Buddy Holly gave his last concert.*

## Homes and Gardens

AMERICAN GOTHIC HOUSE
Gothic St., Eldon, 515-281-7650
*Inspired by its architecture, Grant Wood used this house in his world-famous painting,* American Gothic.

BELLEVUE BUTTERFLY GARDEN
Bellevue State Park, Bellevue, 319-872-4019
*Attracts approximately 60 species of butterflies each year.*

BRUCEMORE
2160 Linden Drive SE, Cedar Rapids, 319-362-7375
*A 26-acre estate that features rolling lawns, a formal garden, and an 1886 21-room Queen Anne–style mansion.*

CEDAR ROCK
2615 Quasqueton Diagonal Blvd., Quasqueton, 319-934-3572
*Completed in 1950, Frank Lloyd Wright's 11-acre Cedar Rock house features his custom-designed furnishings.*

DUBUQUE ARBORETUM/BOTANICAL GARDENS
3800 Arboretum Drive, Dubuque, 319-556-2100
*Award-winning gardens display flowers and vegetables, prairie grasses, wildflowers, and water gardens.*

MAMIE DOUD EISENHOWER BIRTHPLACE
709 Carroll St., Boone, 515-432-1896
*A completely restored frame house with memorabilia.*

DES MOINES BOTANICAL CENTER
909 E. River Dr., Des Moines, 515-242-2934
*Conservatory and large collections of tropical, subtropical, and desert plants.*

IOWA ARBORETUM, INC
1875 Peach Ave., Madrid, Boone
*Walking trails along 300 acres of forest offer views of hundreds of cultivated trees, shrubs, and flowers.*

GLENN MILLER BIRTHPLACE HOME
601 S. Glenn Miller Ave., Clarinda, 712-542-3560
*Tour the home where Alton Glenn Miller was born.*

MONTAUK
Hwy. 18 north of Clermont, Clermont, 319-423-7173
*Home of Iowa's 12th governor, this 1874 brick and native limestone mansion contains all original and historic furnishings.*

TERRACE HILL HISTORIC SITE
2300 Grand Ave., Des Moines, 515-281-3604
*This 1869 opulent Victorian mansion, home of Iowa's first governor, was built by Iowa's first millionaire.*

TODD HOUSE
705 Park St., Tabor, 712-629-2675
*Built in 1853, a station on the Underground Railroad.*

JOHN WAYNE BIRTHPLACE
224 S. Second St., Winterset, 515-462-1044
*Built in the 1880s, the house where Wayne was born is filled with photos and memorabilia from his movie career.*

FRANK LLOYD WRIGHT STOCKMAN HOUSE
530 First St. NE., Mason City, 515-423-1923
*Wright's first Iowa building, designed in 1908.*

## Other Resources

AMANA ARTS GUILD GALLERY
1210 G St., High Amana, 319-622-3678
*Exhibits of handcrafted folk arts produced by Amana artisans.*

STATE CAPITOL
E. Ninth and Grand Ave., Des Moines, 515-281-5591
*Century-old building features a 275-foot gold-leafed dome.*

STATE OF IOWA HISTORICAL BUILDING
600 E. Locust St., Des Moines, 515-281-5111
*In a modern glass and granite building, exhibits of prehistory, natural history, and pioneer life.*

# CREDITS

The authors have made every effort to reach copyright holders of text and owners of illustrations, and wish to thank those individuals and institutions that permitted the reprinting of text or the reproduction of works from their collections. Those credits not listed in the captions are provided below. References are to page numbers; the designations *a*, *b*, and *c* indicate position of illustrations on pages.

## Text

Hal Leonard Corporation: Excerpt from the lyrics to "Iowa Stubborn." Words and Music by Meredith Willson. Copyright © 1957 (Renewed) Frank Music Corp. and Meredith Willson Music. All Rights Reserved.

Harold Matson Co., Inc.: *State Fair*, copyright © 1932 by Phil Stong. Renewed © 1959 by Virginia Swain Stong. By permission of Harold Matson Co. as agent for the estate of Phil Stong.

Iowa REC News: *All Iowa Chowder* by Kathi Pudzuvelis. Used by permission of *Iowa REC News*, May 1995.

Iowa Sesquicentennial Commission: Selection by Mary Swander from *Iowa: A Celebration of Land, People, and Purpose*. Copyright © 1995 Iowa Sesquicentennial Commission. Reprinted by permission.

Iowa State University Press: "Landscape—Iowa," from *Snake in the Strawberries* by James Hearst. Copyright © 1979 by James Hearst.

University of Illinois Press: *Black Heart: An Autobiography* by Black Hawk, edited by Donald Jackson. Copyright © 1990.

University of Iowa Press: *Fragrant Hearts*, by Grace Bouler Forgrave, from *An Iowa Album: A Photographic History* by Mary Bennett. Copyright © 1990. Reprinted by permission of University of Iowa Press. *Vandemark's Folly* by Herbert Quick. Copyright © 1987.

Warner Books: *The Bridges of Madison County* by Robert James Waller. Copyright © 1992. Reprinted by permission of Warner Books, Inc. All rights reserved.

W. W. Norton: *A Bicentennial History* by Joseph Frazier Wall. Copyright © 1978. By permission of W.W. Norton.

Ray A. Young Bear: Lines from "coming back home" from *Winter of the Salamander: The Keeper of Importance* by Ray A. Young Bear. Copyright © 1980 by Ray A. Young Bear.

## Illustrations

AMANA ARTS GUILD: **64b** Apple picker basket; THE ART INSTITUTE OF CHICAGO: **73** *American Gothic* by Grant Wood, 1930. Oil on beaver board. 74.3 x 62.4 cm. Friends of the American Art Collection. 1930.934. © Estate of Grant Wood/Licensed by VAGA, New York, NY; AUTRY MUSEUM OF WESTERN HERITAGE: **39** *American Progress* by John Gast, c. 1850. Oil on canvas. 17¾ x 21½"; **52** *Westward the Star of Empire Takes Its Way—Near Council Bluffs, Iowa* by Andrew Melrose, 1867. Oil on canvas. 25½ x 46"; BIX BIEDERBECKE MEMORIAL SOCIETY: **88**; CONNIE BROTHERS: **79**; COMMUNITY SCHOOL DISTRICT, CEDAR RAPIDS, IOWA: **75b** *Arbor Day* by Grant Wood, 1932. Oil on masonite panel. 24 x 29½". © Estate of Grant Wood/Licensed by VAGA, New York, NY; CORBIS-BETTMAN: **26**; **40a** John Brown; CROWN PUBLISHERS, INC.: **47a** Illustration from *The Complete Book of Fruits and Vegetables* by F. Bianchini and F. Corbetta, illustrated by Marilena Pistoia. Copyright © 1973 by Arnold Mondadori Editore and Crown Publishers, Inc.; DAVENPORT MUSEUM OF ART: **72** *Self-Portrait* by Grant Wood, 1932. Oil on masonite panel. 14¾ x 12¼". © Estate of Grant Wood/Licensed by VAGA, New York, NY; DES MOINES ART CENTER: **60a**; DES MOINES REGISTER AND TRIBUNE CO.: **54a**; **54b** Brian Duffy cartoon courtesy the artist; DREASLER PHOTOGRAPHY: **78a** Portrait of Samuel Clemens; ELVEHJEM MUSEUM OF ART: **74b** *Portrait of Nan* by Grant Wood, 1933. Oil on masonite. 34½ x 28½". © Estate of Grant Wood/Licensed by VAGA, New York, NY; THE FINE ARTS MUSEUMS OF SAN FRANCISCO: **74–75a** *Dinner for Threshers* by Grant Wood, 1934. Oil on hardboard. 20 x 80". Gift of Mr. and Mrs. John D. Rockefeller 3rd, 1979. 7.105. © Estate of Grant Wood/Licensed by VAGA, New York, NY; GLENN MILLER BIRTHPLACE SOCIETY: **83a**; HOMSTAD STUDIO & GALLERY, Decorah, Iowa: **5** *In the Garden* by Carl Homstad, 1993. Woodcut. 8½ x 9¼"; ILLINOIS HISTORIC PRESERVATION AGENCY: **15a** Portrait of Black Hawk by Charles Bird King, c. 1833–37. Hauberg Indian Museum, Black Hawk State Historic Site; INDEPENDENCE NATIONAL HISTORICAL PARK: **37b** Major Stephen Harriman Long by Charles Willson Peale, c. 1819. Oil on canvas. 24¼ x 20¼"; IOWA DEPT. OF TRANSPORTATION: **15b** Sesquicentennial license plate; JASPER COUNTY HISTORICAL SOCIETY: **86a** Maytag washer; JOSLYN ART MUSEUM, OMAHA, NEBRASKA: **20–21** *View on the Missouri* by Karl Bodmer, 1833. Watercolor on paper. 6⅜ x 10⅜". Gift of the Enron Art Foundation; LIBRARY OF CONGRESS: **35a** Zebulon Pike; **44** Farm Security Administration photograph by Russell Lee, 1936; GARY R. LUCY GALLERIES: **53a** *The Omaha: Westward Travels on the Missouri River, 1856* by Gary R. Lucy, 1993. Oil on canvas. 8 x 12"; MADISON COUNTY CHAMBER OF COMMERCE: **59c** Hogback Bridge; MAMIE DOUD EISENHOWER BIRTHPLACE HOME: **63b** Mamie Doud Eisenhower and birthplace interior; VICTOR MCCULLOUGH: **84a** *Midway*, 1994. Acrylic and colored pencil on panel. 12 x 48". Collection Dr. Ron and Mary Pick; WILL MENTOR: **85** *Reclamation of a Small Waste Area*, 1996. Oil on wood. 33 x 24". Collection Laura and Mark Adler; METRO OPERA COMPANY OF DES MOINES: **82** Photo John F. Schultz; WENDELL MINOR: **69**; MOUNT MERCY COLLEGE: **57b, c** Lincoln Highway postcard and game. Photo David Van Allen; MUSCATINE ART CENTER, MUSCATINE, IOWA: **8** *View of the Mississippi from Wyoming Hill* by William E. L. Bunn, 1946. Oil on canvas. 20 x 26½". Gift of Raymond Titus; **61** *Prayer of Peace* by Allen Houser, 1987. Bronze. 124½ x 32 x 49". Gift of Helen and Stanley Howell, in memory of C. Maxwell Stanley; NATIONAL ARCHIVES AT COLLEGE PARK, MARYLAND: **18**; NATIONAL ARCHIVES OF CANADA: **16a**; **34** *Discovery of the Mississippi by Marquette A.D. 1673* by J. N. Marchand, 1903. Color photomechanical print in light card. 25.5 x 17 cm. PA-237054; NATIONAL GEOGRAPHIC SOCIETY IMAGE COLLECTION: **12a** Iowa flag, illustration by Marilyn Dye Smith; **12b** Wild rose and eastern goldfinch, illustration by Robert E. Hynes; NATIONAL MUSEUM OF AMERICAN ART/ART RESOURCE: **30** *Little Wolf, a famous warrior* by George Catlin, 1844. Oil on canvas; **31b** *Keokuk on Horseback* by George Catlin. Oil on canvas. 24 x 29"; NATIONAL PARK SERVICE: **29a** Effigy mounds; NEW YORK PUBLIC LIBRARY: **13a** White oak, engraving by August Plée from the drawing by Pierre-Joseph Redouté in *Histoire des Chenes de l'Amerique*, 1801; NEW YORK STATE MUSEUM: **24**; NORTH CAROLINA MUSEUM OF ART: **26** *Spring on the Missouri* by Thomas Hart Benton, 1945. 30¼ x 40¼". © T. H. Benton and R. P. Benton Testamentary Trusts/Licensed by VAGA, New York, NY; GENIE HUDSON PATRICK: **35b** *Various Points*. Oil on paper. 20 x 28"; PHOTOFEST: **70, 81**; PHOTO RESEARCHERS: **12c** Geode. Photo E. R. Degginger. National Audubon Society Collection; KEN REGAN/CAMERA FIVE: **59a, b** By permission of National Geographic Society; SIOUX CITY PUBLIC MUSEUM:

**49** *Corn Palace*. Photographer unknown; LE SPEARMAN: **87c** Keebler Tree; STAMP KING: **14a** Iowa centennial stamp; STATE HISTORICAL SOCIETY OF IOWA: **17a** Cap Anson; **32b** Detail of silk appliqué sash; **33**; **37a** *Engineer Cantonment with Deer* by Titian Ramsay Peale, 1822. Watercolor on canvas; **38**; **40b** Eleventh Iowa Infantry Band; **50–51**; **57a** Civil War veterans; **67a** Four-patch quilt. Cotton. 71½ x 77¾"; **67b** Carved duck; **68a** Cap Anson; **76a, b**; **77** Town drop, from the collections of the Museum of Repertoire Americana; **83b** Keota Ladies' Band; STATE OF IOWA: **13b** State seal; SUPERSTOCK: **17b** Herbert Hoover; TABOR HISTORICAL SOCIETY: **41** Sketch of the Todd House by William Wagner; TATE GALLERY, LONDON/ART RESOURCE, NY: **78b** *The Name of Dante Gabriel Rossetti is heard for the First Time in the Western States of America* by Sir Max Beerbohm, 1882 (cartoon of Oscar Wilde). Watercolor; TIME INC.: **55** Time cover © 1948. Reprinted by permission; UNIVERSITY OF IOWA MUSEUM OF ART: **31a** Miniature cradle with human effigy, c. 1900. Wood, bone, German silver brooches, native leather, paint, glass beads, wool, and printed cotton cloth. 17" h. Private collection; **32a** Mesquakie cuffs owned by Gerald "Tuffy" Svacina, c. 1925. Glass beads, native leather, cotton cloth. 7 x 13½"; **43** *Corn Country* by Lee Allen, 1937. Oil on canvas. Gift of Dr. Clarence Van Epps; UNIVERSITY OF IOWA, STATE ARCHEOLOGIST: **29b** Bear claw necklace; VESTERHEIM NORWEGIAN-AMERICAN MUSEUM: **45a** Wooden spoons by Erik Tiegen (1842–1902). Hand-carved wood; WALLACES' FARMER: **71b** Duroc boar; MIKE WHYE: **86b** Hot air-balloon over Indianola, **86c** Little Brown Church, **87a** Coffeepot, **87b** Grotto, **89**; MARTHA YODER: **84b** *Marvin's Barn*, 1996. Intaglio. 18 x 15"

## Acknowledgments

Walking Stick Press wishes to thank our project staff: Miriam Lewis, Laurie Donaldson, Georgia Finnigan, Daniel Golden, Adam Ling, and Catherine Scott.

For other assistance with *Iowa*, we are especially grateful to: Laurel Anderson/Photosynthesis, David Cavagnaro, Lindsay Kefauver/Visual Resources, Deborah Leveton of the Des Moines Art Center, Shaner Magalhães of the State Historical Society of Iowa, Steven Orhn, Le Spearman, and Mike Whye.